TURNING DARKNESS INTO LIGHT

Inspiring Lessons After
A Near-Suicide

Dr. S. L. Young

Copyright © 2016, 2020 - 2023
Beyond SPRH, LLC   Arlington, VA

Version 2.2

All rights reserved. No part of this book may be reproduced in any manner or transmitted in any form without written approval from the author. The only exception is the inclusion of a brief quotation with the source acknowledged.

ISBN-13: 978-1515239062
ISBN-10: 1515239063

Library of Congress Control Number: 2015912142

Dedications

<u>To my mom:</u> I learned from your incredible strength, determination, and ability to make things happen against great odds. You ingrained in me the skills to learn ways to move mountains. The many tough and invaluable lessons you taught me saved my life.

<u>To my brother (Johnnie):</u> Thank you for saving my life! Your recognition of my medical emergency is the only reason I didn't end my life in March 2014. I can never repay you for the gift of having a second chance to begin again. The best way to demonstrate my thankfulness and gratitude to you is to continue to relentlessly serve others to help them to be and do better, too.

<u>To my sister (Joyce):</u> Thank you for the comforting words during my mental health crisis. Your calm words helped me to systematically reboot, refocus and determine the initial steps to identify a positive path forward.

<u>To Virginia Clay (my muse):</u> During the early days of my depression, you unknowingly uplifted my self-esteem and confidence. This helped me to believe that the seemingly impossible could be my reality.

<u>To Brian Marhefsky:</u> You convinced me to do the hardest thing I've ever done, which was to maintain my commitment to teach inmates within a few hours of me wanting to die. By pushing me forward, I took the first steps to reclaim my life and began to further my dedication to community outreach.

<u>To Virginia Smith:</u> Fortunately, you returned to my life at a critical time that my soul was crumbling. During those turbulent years, you encouraged, supported, and loved me. Also, you communicated through your vision and insight that my work was valuable. Furthermore, you directed me toward bigger audiences that led to unimaginable personal and professional successes, which didn't just help me… it helped many others, too. Therefore, my numerous accomplishments should be claimed by you, as if you did it yourself. Please always know that I am the man I am today because you told me who I was before I realized who I could be. For this and so much more, I am forever grateful.

<u>To Brian Hanson:</u> I didn't meet you in the physical world, but your life and mine will always be connected. Thanks for sharing our (your natural and my adopted) mother with me. We are brothers in spirit who are extremely blessed to have a loving, compassionate, caring, and supportive mom.

<u>To Mary Hanson:</u> I'm saddened that we met due to our shared journeys related to the negative impacts of depression, mental health, and suicide. However, I'm incredibly blessed that we are connected. If it weren't for your ongoing encouragement, kindness, support, and love during a critical five-year period, then I might have surrendered to the darkness and unnecessarily ended my life. You are now my friend and second mother, but since the day we met you were and will always be my angel on earth.

Table of Contents

Foreword by Mary Hanson 10

Message from the Author – Dr. S. L. Young 12

Preface 15

Depression – An Unnecessary Stigma 20

Depression: It Happens! 25

Helping Someone Who Might Be Depressed 27

Functioning While Depressed 30

Depression: Coming Out of the Fog 33

The Day I Almost Committed Suicide 37

Depression Can Be a Limiter: Willpower a Liberator 42

Depression as a Mnemonic 46

Letter to Myself the Day Before My Near-Suicide: Written a Year Later 48

Depression: My Journey Through the Fog 54

Someone Stopped and Listened; It's the Only Reason I'm Still Alive 58

Depression Can Lead to Individuals Questioning Their Value(s) 63

Journey After a Near-Suicide to Educate, Remove Stigmas, and Save Lives 69

What If?! 72

It's Still a Wonderful Life 77

High School Friends; Different Ethical Paths; Almost Identical Tragic Endings 83

Defending Robin Williams' Death and Leveraging Facebook Helped Me to Rediscover My Light 88

Parting Thoughts 94

Epilogue 97

Sharing Pain Leads to Building New Family Connections 100

Reflections on My Battle to Save and Reclaim My Life 110

A Second Chance at Life Led to Learning Ways to Purposefully Live 117

Letter to Myself the Day Before My Near-Suicide Written Almost Seven Years Later 128

The Long-Awaited Meeting with an Angel 137

An Unexpected and Welcomed Surprise Visit 143

Parting Thoughts: Part Two 145

Appendix A: Laws Protect Certain Classes from Workplace Abuse: Why Not Everyone? 150

Appendix B: Belief: An Underutilized Tool 154

Appendix C: The Presentation that Changed and Saved My Life 159

Appendix D: Are You Really Who You Think You Are?! 161

Appendix E: Why Shouldn't Men Cry?! 166

Appendix F: Becoming a Better Man 171

Appendix G: Inmate Management: What's Wanted Better Criminals or Citizens? 177

About the Author 185

Foreword by Mary Hanson

My son (Brian) unexpectedly chose to end his life on February 9, 2012, one week and a day before his 27th birthday. Brian's death caused our family to grieve, drove us to understand the reasons for it, and began an incredibly painful journey to heal which continues to this day. A large part of my personal journey involved immersing myself in numerous written materials that dealt with suicide, mental health, and spirituality.

Stacey L. Young (Sly, as I have come to know him) and I connected as we separately attempted to heal from the impacts of depression. Sly was trying to recover from his near-suicide in 2014 and I was trying to rationalize the reasons that caused my son to end his life.

In 2015, while perusing my daily news fix on the Huffington Post, a blog post entitled "Letter to Myself the Day Before My Near Suicide – Written a Year Later" jumped-off my iPad's screen. This article took me on an emotional journey. The minute-by-minute recounting of a dark, pivotal day in which he ultimately chose life over suicide mesmerized me. Sly's descriptive abilities were so strong that I couldn't help but relate them back to my son, and the things he endured that awful night. The parallels were heartbreaking, informative, and provided valuable insights about the impacts of depression on mental health.

This article haunted me. My feelings were so strong that I was moved to contact him to share my appreciation and provide my thanks for sharing his life with readers. NEVER did I ever imagine that he would respond. Yet, within hours, he wrote to me and then… a close friendship began.

S. L. Young, in this book, provides an amazingly vulnerable and personal perspective about depression, suicide, and recovery.

"Turning Darkness Into Light" is a brief but mighty book. It's full of serendipitous moments and practical information for anyone who struggles with depression, as well as for the loved ones who support someone who is depressed.

Over the past seven years, Sly has strived to live a purposeful life by committing himself to supporting and educating those in need generally and who have mental health challenges specifically. As a lifelong learner and most prominently an educator, he leverages his second chance in life to make a positive difference to encourage others to seek various options to save their lives, too.

This book, for me, is magical and hopeful. It reinforces a couple of core spiritual beliefs that I hold dear. First, in this life, there are no accidents or mistakes. Second, by taking positive chances, no matter the size, these actions can propel you forward toward even more positive experiences and connections. Third, by being open about our struggles, opportunities to connect, heal, and begin again can (and do) happen. This last point led Sly and me to help each other heal, save each other, and create an extended family that's filled with love.

Thank you, S. L. Young, for being someone who tenaciously participates in life, a caring teacher, an unbounded creator, and most of all a beloved friend/son.

Message from the Author – Dr. S. L. Young

Depression isn't something that I thought would happen to me. I'm usually a positive and high energy guy. Although, I've had moments of sadness, disappointment, anger, disbelief, and more. These feelings normally happened... and in a few days or so I was back to normal.

After repeatedly receiving very nasty, harsh, and retaliatory attacks for doing things that I was trained to do as a good person and prudent businessman, such as: treating others with respect, not being unethical, and not being complicit to workplace bullying. These normally positive behaviors continually led to negative outcomes for me.

As a result, I questioned my values, the correctness of my actions, the costs I was willing to pay for success, and the commitment I had to my morals and values. These internal considerations subsequently led to feeling devalued, demoralized, dejected, and sometimes disgusted not by my actions, but by the lack of civility, ethics, and standards of human decency by others.

At the onset of negative thoughts and considerations related to these feelings, I started to enter an extended period of depression. Then, over time, my situation didn't get any better, my mental state continued to deteriorate, and at an unplanned moment in which I lost all hope that things would ever get any better... I finalized my exit strategy, made my planned final call, and was a few moments from ending my life.

Until depression affected me, no one proactively discussed the topic of depression with me, which is extremely unfortunate. I was aware of the word, understood that it had negative impacts, but I didn't understand the causes, symptoms, or impacts.

Depression isn't something that individuals should learn about once it happens to them. There are plenty of conversations throughout our lives about the functions of the body ranging from uses, development, and potential health issues that might affect its proper operation. Conversely, there are seldom (if ever) any orchestrated discussions during an adolescent's developmental years about the importance of mental health or its potential issues.

Learning about something (such as depression) that might negatively impact someone's ability to function, cope, be productive, or happy should be integrated into other health discussions in school (age appropriate) about human anatomy and biology. This way individuals will learn about methods to recognize mental health challenges long before the impact(s) of these changes adversely impacts their (and sometimes others') lives.

It's well past time that stigmas and negative labels (e.g., weak, crazy) associated with depression be eliminated so that anyone who might be affected by this sometimes-debilitating medical issue doesn't feel any embarrassment, harassment, or reservations about seeking treatment for a bona fide health condition.

The time is now to stop classifying, judging, and evaluating someone's personal or private medical challenges (regardless of the source, impact, or physical characteristics) to ensure that everyone who needs and/or wants to obtain treatment does so without reservation.

If you have feelings that might not seem normal, don't be afraid to ask for assistance. If you have any concerns about your well-being, please get examined. If someone needs to talk to you about their challenges, please promise yourself that you will stop and listen to their concerns and provide support… as a single conversation might save someone's life.

No one should die due to worries about someone's assessment(s) about their ability to cope, strength (physical or mental), or any other unnecessary judgmental classifications.

The issue isn't that someone has a physical or mental ailment that might need medical attention. The real issue is that anyone is caused to feel bad, judged, or harassed about their situation, belief(s), or choice(s), which might delay or prevent them from obtaining the help needed to get and be better.

Preface

The personal essays contained herein were written during the year following my disclosure to family and friends that I battled depression. I was recovering after my near-suicide in March 2014, along with publicly sharing my mental health experiences on the Maggie Linton Show[1] in August 2014. Prior to these disclosures, I knew I would share my journey with depression at some point. However, I didn't know the timeframe.

I was compelled to counter judgmental comments about depression and suicide (after a friend-of-a-friend on Facebook) questioned the reason that anyone would take their life after Robin Williams' death-by-suicide. At first, I provided a general defense that no one should make senseless judgments about someone's reasons to end their life, as only the affected individual understood the demons that led to their decision.

The next day I mustered the courage to share my mental health challenges with family and friends. This decision was one of the hardest things I've ever done. However, it's also the best thing I've ever done. Making my decision to disclose my near-suicide allowed me to release unnecessary stress related to worrying about if someone learned about my struggles or the internal turmoil of trying to behave as if everything was okay during conversations... while things weren't going well.

---

[1] Dr. Young disclosed his battle with depression and journey to recover after a near-suicide (to a national audience) on the Maggie Linton Show on 8/18/14: youtu.be/dUi2IQxcHrM

Even though I wrote my book "Choosing To Take A Stand: Changed me, my life, and my destiny[2]" about the reasons for my near-suicide a couple of months after that fateful day. This writing (and reflective experience) was completed because I recognized the immense importance of capturing my unfiltered, raw, and emotional thoughts to help others.

I couldn't have imagined that my journey would be shared so boldly and publicly, but if my story saves a life then it's well worth any personal costs or judgements about me (related to sharing my journey and battle with depression or others questioning my coping skills).

Shortly after reading my book Choosing To Take A Stand prior to its release, a very close friend directed me to never publish it. This friend's advice was to keep my written record as a private journal for my personal use and not public consumption.

Even though this friend expressed her reservations about releasing my work, I was committed to raising awareness about depression (specifically) and mental health (generally), as both topics are too many times unnecessarily considered to be societal taboos and not something that should be a topic of discussion until someone famous dies by suicide.

I don't know (and might not ever know) the reason(s) that I took this enormous leap of faith that led to a year-long writing project. Nevertheless, I do know that my decision to publish

---

[2] This book details Dr. Young's thoughts, considerations, and actions taken to rebuild his life on purpose, with passion, and with a new perspective after his near-suicide in March 2014.

my initial book which shared my experience with depression and to also continue to write about this topic (without any concerns about being evaluated or judged) changed my life.

The most unexpected benefits related to sharing my private battle with depression publicly were the outpouring of support, understanding, compassion, and encouragement. Yet, the comments that made me really understand the significance of my work were the private stories that were shared with me, such as:

1. The many positive messages and personal stories received from individuals (including close friends) who privately shared their battles with depression;
2. A parent who told me that by sharing my story it helped her to have a better understanding about the way her son's final hours might have gone;
3. The woman who strengthened my resolve to continue to discuss my journey. She shared with me that she never understood the reason that her husband made a final call to his cousin prior to his suicide (he ended his life approximately twenty-two years ago) until she read details about my story.

The year following my near-suicide wasn't perfect. However, by choosing to live and being willing to release my pain, I began to heal myself and (surprisingly) helped others to be and do better too.

In March 2014, I didn't want to die; I just desperately wanted the pain to go away!!!

I am forever grateful for:

- **my brother, Johnnie** – who recognized my medical emergency and relentlessly worked to redirect my suicidal-thoughts;

- **my sister, Joyce** – who provided unimaginable support during the trying years following my near-suicide;

- **my other family members and friends** – who offered to be available if the suicidal thoughts returned;

- **the countless others** – who shared their love and support during those very trying times.

My message to anyone who struggles with any mental health challenges is… please seek help and don't give-up on life. As long as you're alive, there are various opportunities for things to get and be better (even if the possibilities don't seem to be very likely at the moment).

I never could've imagined that by actively choosing to live that I would help myself and many others, too. The most unlikely surprise is that I created a life for myself that's more purposeful and meaningful now than I could have ever conceived.

As my brother said to me during my mental health emergency, "Stacey, this is just a moment; you need to get past this moment."

It's my sincere hope that my story can and will help others to have the strength to recover and persevere, too.

For me, I couldn't see a future for myself on that fateful day, but I now understand that my life's purpose is much greater than a challenging moment (even if it requires me to push past my ego's concerns about potential embarrassment).

Best wishes on your journey; don't forget to always be *your* best!

Note: Essays in this book were mostly written by the author during periods of significant depression and while battling suicidal thoughts. The writing is mostly in its original format and not overly edited to maintain its authenticity. Notwithstanding, corrections were made for readability and clarity purposes.

If you or someone you know needs assistance, then please contact the Suicide & Crisis Lifeline at:

- 988
- 988lifeline.org

Depression – An Unnecessary Stigma

Depression is an ailment that affects the body just like any other illness. The difference with depression is that it primarily impacts an individual's mind, emotions, outlook, and attitude. Manifestations of depression are similar to those that might be created by other bodily ailments; however, attitudes about depression are usually associated with an individual being weak or lacking an ability to cope instead of being a legitimate medical issue that requires treatment.

After learning about Robin Williams' death, I happened to do a cursory review of my Facebook timeline. It was at this moment I became alarmed and disturbed by a judgmental question made about the reason for his death. This question basically asked, "How could anyone give-up on life since we're all in this together?"

This question was disturbing to me as it's this type of commentary that prevents many individuals who suffer from depression from disclosing it. Furthermore, insensitive, and naïve comments compound the difficulty individuals have to admit any mental health challenge, begin treatment, and prevent unnecessary negative outcomes.

My response to this Facebook message was, Life has so many ebbs and flows. It's very difficult to know the way someone is feeling on the inside as oftentimes individuals are fighting a private battle that no one else knows anything about it. Then, individuals are shocked because they never saw it coming. Well sometimes these individuals (like me recently) don't see it coming either and wake-up with it already inside of them, as it's not a part of them. Therefore, whether you know of someone's internal battles or not, if something appears to be different, ask them questions and don't be afraid to ask. As that moment of hesitation may be the last moment that might keep that individual alive. Once an individual is gone isn't the time to speculate about the potential reasons, the time to speculate and ask questions is now… before it's too late. Rest in peace, Robin Williams!

In responding to this post, I did something that I needed to do but couldn't previously determine a way to communicate my battle with depression. Once I self-identified the issue in 2012 and during my recovery, I wrote, prayed, and used very controlled disclosures about my mental health challenges. After the insensitive Facebook remark about Mr. Williams' suicide, I shared publicly for the first-time information about my battles with depression. Prior to this personal disclosure, the biggest barriers to my inability to communicate my legitimate medical challenges were related to unnecessary fears about sharing my struggles which heightened my level of depression, a concern about others' perceptions about me if this information was revealed, and the stigma associated with admitting to being depressed (even to myself).

After indirectly disclosing that I had considered ending my life, I decided to go even further to reveal to my Facebook family and friends that I had been depressed and moments from committing suicide. Part of the message shared was "There's never a good way to share bad news; however, I will be direct. My life has been absolutely miserable for the past 2 1/2 years due to a situation that was out-of-my-control. This issue caused me to go into periods of deep depression, uncontrolled emotional outbursts, and this last March I was moments from committing suicide. I wrote my post yesterday about not knowing someone's challenges (related to Robin Williams) because it directly relates to me; the smiles and happiness I pretended to have were just my outward attempt to cope with desperation and despair."

The amount of concern and support received after my public disclosure was overwhelming. A response received via a private Facebook message from a former student was especially jolting,

> Hi, I don't know if you remember me, but you as my professor made such an impact on my life, you have no idea. You have so many students in and out of your classroom every year and your story resonates with each of them. My son, who was suffering from depression and severe anxiety, finally this past month got a job and is working full-time. He is connecting with old friends and is talking about going back to school. I kept impressing upon him your story and showing him your books. I know it made difference. ... You my dear friend would be missed, I hope you realize that. And the stamp you left in my life and thus the life of those I touch is never ending.

This type of message is great, but the challenge is that most times similar messages are communicated after someone is badly hurt or dead. This is a significant reason that it's critical that individuals slow down, share their love for others now, and occasionally don't be afraid to ask if someone is okay --- especially if there are noticeable changes in their appearance, habits, attitudes, or activities.

Mental health concerns shouldn't be viewed as a weakness, but instead as an urgent medical need. Therefore, let's collectively remove the unnecessary and preventable shame that is created by making anyone feel that any type of medical condition is a weakness, including mental health challenges such as depression.

As for me, the only reason that I didn't commit suicide that day was because of my mother. The day I was going to commit suicide, I called my brother Johnnie[3] (while trying to keep my emotions in check) to ensure that he would take care of our mother if I was unable to do so. Fortunately for me two things happened: (1) I broke down during our call and (2) my brother started asking questions, kept calling back after I hung up the phone, and made me face my own reality by telling me to use the advice in my books to help myself. If my brother hadn't recognized my medical emergency, asked questions immediately, demonstrated love and support, I'm certain that I wouldn't be alive today to share my story.

I didn't want to share my story, but it's important to do so anyway. Not only for my recovery, but by making these public disclosures I hope to inspire others to not feel embarrassed, ashamed, or fearful by also communicating that they're struggling and need help.

Remember, from the day we're born until the day we're buried, we don't do anything alone. Therefore, don't be afraid to disclose your struggles and ask for help. Being vulnerable to share your challenges isn't a weakness but instead a strength; the challenge many times is convincing yourself otherwise.

---

[3] Listen to a powerful and lifesaving discussion about the day that Dr. Young's brother (Johnnie) saved his life: youtu.be/yGlQVWq75bE

As for Robin Williams, your body of work will help so many others who will watch your many artistic masterpieces to help make themselves better. You didn't find your peace while alive, but in your untimely ending you have helped me to rediscover mine. Your tragic ending is unfortunate, but my renewed strength is because of your personal sacrifice, which will allow me to now help many others because of you.

Robin Williams… May God bless you, your family, and all those who loved your spirit, your work, and you.

Depression: It Happens!

There is sometimes confusion about mental health challenges, as well as a lack of understanding about depression as compared to other bodily ailments. Depression is an issue related to the body's functioning and should be addressed similar to any other medical condition. Depression can be associated with irregular brain activity, a chemical imbalance, or a situational event (single or periodic).

There are times that (despite available information) individuals will believe things that might not be true, even if there isn't any evidence to support the belief. Usually, these beliefs are related to an individual's emotions, such as feeling insecure, being jealous, having self-doubt, or making unnecessary comparisons. These types of feelings aren't necessarily related to irregular brain activity, as emotions (sometimes irrational) are a normal part of human existence. However, if these feelings lead to an individual engaging in harmful thoughts or behaviors (to themselves or others), then this may be the beginning of a medical concern.

Sometimes the body doesn't function as it should because of an imbalance, such as a lack of water, sleep, nutrients, or other factors. During these times, an individual might not think clearly, be as productive, might feel sluggish, or may experience other noticeable differences. Individuals who seek relief from these types of imbalances will usually need to take corrective action to restore their body to its normal functioning. Similar imbalances can occur for individuals who are affected or effected by depression caused by a chemical imbalance. For these individuals, the body lacks the ability to adjust on its own; therefore, individuals may use medicine to adjust the body's chemistry.

A life event can also cause a sudden change in an individual's attitude, mood, or beliefs. These changes aren't related to irregular brain activity or a chemical imbalance but are related to a situational event. For example, someone might experience a headache after a stressful day and will either allow the pain to subside on its own or will take pain medication to obtain relief. Another individual might experience headaches throughout the year related to their internal chemistry, specific events, or environmental conditions, which may require a pain management strategy. These comparisons highlight the difference between single versus periodic events that can occur for someone who isn't always depressed.

An individual's depression can have various origins, which need to be identified to develop an effective management plan. Depression whether related to irregular brain activity, a chemical imbalance, or a life event shouldn't be considered a weakness, an inability to cope, or any other judgmental evaluation.

Depression is a legitimate medical concern that affects and causes effects to the body. Therefore, depression symptoms should be identified, treated, and managed similar to any other medical condition that might impact anyone's ability to function and experience a fulfilled life.

Helping Someone Who Might Be Depressed

Individuals who might be depressed could use attention, support, a conversation, an outing, and more. However, something that isn't needed is for someone to say… "It could be much worse," "Some people can't get out of bed," or "People in third-world countries don't have clean drinking water." All these things might be true, but none of these things have anything to do with an individual who feels depressed. These evaluative comments are a comparison about the legitimacy of someone's depression relative to something that isn't a justifiable reference point.

Suggestions (based on my experiences) to help someone who might be depressed:

- Don't Make Assumptions – An individual might have something that bothers their mental well-being but might not be ready for help or to disclose their feelings. An interested party might have a concern that something is wrong, but an emotional disclosure about the source of an individual's pain cannot be forced. However, you can let someone know that you're available to provide support.

- Offer Assistance - Ask if there's anything the person wants to discuss. Then, wait for a response. This type of inquiry demonstrates that someone is interested in their well-being. Then, if someone doesn't want to answer or doesn't respond, then don't force the communication. Instead, wait until a later time to ask again, but don't harass them to disclose something there isn't a readiness to discuss.

- <u>Don't Be Judgmental</u> - A challenge with disclosing emotional challenges can be related to others' judgments or the stigma sometimes associated with depression. Affected individuals can be incorrectly labeled as being weak, lacking coping skills, or some other evaluative comment. Therefore, don't provide any commentary that might make anyone feel evaluated; instead, make an individual feel comfortable that there isn't anything that can't be or should make themselves feel ashamed to discuss.

- <u>Allow for Disclosures on Their Own Time</u> - An individual might not be ready to disclose information about something that makes them feel depressed at that moment, but that doesn't mean that there won't be a desire to do so in the future.

- <u>Let Them Tell Their Story</u> – It can be difficult for someone to move past the challenge(s) to disclose a personal struggle with depression or something else; therefore, once someone starts to tell their story ... try to be an extra good listener. This will allow an individual to share anything that there is comfort in sharing without having to think through responses to questions (at least at that moment). This approach will allow an individual to freely release information as much as desired, as questions can be delayed until a later time. Also, an inappropriate question may cause an individual to stop disclosing information and even worse might prevent further information from being shared.

- <u>Nothing but Unconditional Support</u> – The goal is to help someone who is depressed, which means providing unconditional support without judging. The issues that caused an individual to become depressed might not be important to someone inquiring, but the issue is still significant to the affected individual. Therefore, once the conversation starts, remove any judgments, assumptions, analysis, or closed-minded thoughts to have an open discussion.

Depression is a personal battle, but it doesn't have to and shouldn't be fought alone. An effective strategy to help someone who faces a personal challenge is to provide unconditional support to resolve any issue(s) during their recovery.

Functioning While Depressed

Depression isn't necessarily related to individuals who aren't able to function, as there are numerous individuals who are depressed (whether they know it or not) and manage their daily affairs. These individuals (like me in the past) maintain their daily activities but may also struggle with an undisclosed personal challenge.

Individuals who are depressed don't often readily admit it to others or themselves. Many times, individuals won't make this admission because these types of disclosures can lead to the receipt of negative commentary related to an affected party being weak, crazy, or not having coping skills. These negative references are a significant factor that many individuals don't seek help (professional or otherwise) and often self-medicate.

The origin of an individual's depression can be related to:

- psychological - irregular brain activity;
- physiological - a chemical imbalance;
- situational - a specific event;
- periodic - certain time periods (e.g., death, anniversary of a divorce, something else).

Knowledge about these variations in the origin of depression is an important starting point to gain a better understanding and to make a quicker determination about an individual who might be affected by depression.

It's also important to note that there are many different manifestations of depression.

Individuals who are depressed might have or experience:

- withdrawal - decreased involvement or a complete halt with activities that an individual normally enjoys;

- sleeping pattern changes - sleep schedule is erratic and/or an individual is sleep deprived;

- substance abuse - use of prescribed drugs or self-medication to deal with the emotional effect of depression;

- excessive activities - distractions to keep themselves occupied (e.g., overeating, constant exercise, increased sexual activity, compulsive cleaning, overworking).

Anyone who experiences health related challenges shouldn't be further stigmatized by negative commentary, attitudes, or behaviors.

Depression is a medical condition that should be treated, which isn't any different than addressing other bodily ailments. If someone feels bad due to a pain in the body, the individual won't normally receive negative commentary (e.g., being a wimp, needing to be tougher) based on the disclosure. This type of understanding and sensitivity should be applied to mental health ailments, too. Anyone who makes someone feel inferior due to any medical issue(s) places an unnecessary stigma and burden on an individual who might otherwise seek professional and/or familial assistance (if their medical concerns weren't considered a shortcoming).

An individual might appear to function normally, however,

there's a noticeable difference or a suspicion that something is wrong. In these times, anyone who has concerns about someone's behavior should ask if there are any issues that might need to be discussed. This moment of concern may make the difference between someone who unnecessarily suffers alone, gets medical attention, discovers an outlet for their stress, or in worst cases prevents someone from committing suicide. It doesn't take a lot of time to actively demonstrate that someone cares and that an individual doesn't have to suffer alone.

Mental health issues cover a spectrum ranging from something that might only affect someone for a few hours or days to something that is more comprehensive that might be dealt with for weeks, months, or years. No matter the severity of the mental health issue(s), there shouldn't be any unnecessary barriers (from individuals or societies) that might prevent someone from seeking medical assistance.

It's time as a society that we collectively "choose to take a stand" about mental health issues, including depression. The change that's needed starts with the ability to have open and honest conversations about mental health issues that can change and save lives. Otherwise, someone you love might unnecessarily suffer due to misplaced concerns about others' beliefs or attitudes versus seeking treatment for a legitimate medical condition.

Depression: Coming Out of the Fog

I'm often asked about my ability to make positive forward-progress after a near suicide. The questions normally asked are: what changed; what drives your ability to persevere?

My usual answer is I simply decided to move forward, despite having severe depression. This response is frustrating to some, but it truthfully describes my action. However, upon further consideration, the drivers of my ability to begin my healing process are more complex.

Details of my journey to recover from depression and a near-suicide:

- First, I recognized that something about me was different. During this initial awareness, there wasn't a complete understanding about the manifestations of these changes; although, something didn't feel normal.

- Second, I started to write to proactively manage the differences and growing distress I felt throughout my body --- especially in my mind. This was an important step because it allowed me to process, analyze, and address some of the unrecognizable feelings that started to grow stronger.

- Third, a critical step that almost came too late, I sought help ... but it wasn't for me. As my mother's caregiver, I needed to ensure that my mom would be taken care of once I was gone. This action also did something I didn't plan, which was to disclose (to someone who cared about me) that I was experiencing a medical emergency (e.g., mental, emotional, psychological distress).

- Fourth, after some of my siblings became aware of my medical emergency, I disclosed the reason for my severe depression, along with my feelings of desperation and despair. These disclosures helped me to release the enormous stress that I hadn't previously shared, which had the added benefit of allowing me to decompress from my mental, emotional, and physical distress.

- Fifth, I wrote my book "Choosing to Take a Stand: Changed me, my life, and my destiny" to heal myself, document my journey, analyze my capabilities, and to help others who have faced or are facing similar challenges. This step was important because it allowed me to analyze and address my life challenges that led to my near-suicide, but more importantly it initiated the process used to heal myself and start to engage with others socially again.

- Sixth, a Facebook friend of a friend wrote a judgmental comment about the reasons an individual would give-up on life after Robin Williams' suicide. My reaction to this comment led to a soft disclosure about my depression to family and friends. Then, the next day, I went even further to make a detailed disclosure about my depression and near-suicide. This was a significant moment that allowed me to release additional and unnecessary stress related to wondering about others' considerations about my depression, along with the circumstances that led to my legitimate medical emergency.

After my challenges were shared publicly, I immediately felt better and the best that I had in years. These sudden mental, emotional, and physical improvements were because I was no longer burdened by internal stress and conflict, which were related to worrying about others' opinions about my medical challenges. Moreover, the support received from friends and family was overwhelming. This also caused me to remember something that I should have already known, which was that I was loved and wasn't alone --- and I didn't have to deal with my life challenges by myself.

- <u>Seventh</u>, I did something a week later that I couldn't have ever imagined, I disclosed my battle with depression and near-suicide to a national radio audience. My ability to widely share my story allowed me to further release my stress. At this point, I was no longer tormented by a major source of my depression, which was the secrecy. By being vulnerable, I removed personal barriers and limitations to discover the courage to allow myself to share my story while I began my recovery.

The sixth and seventh points are significant and life altering for me because individuals who battle depression or their loved ones started to contact me about dealing with depression. These contacts from individuals who needed assistance helped me to realize that by being vulnerable about my mental health challenges, I helped others, too. This realization gave my life a greater purpose, significance, and reasons not to give-up on my life.

By sharing my struggles, I'm now doing something that I couldn't have imagined a short time ago... helping others on their journey to resolve their or others' depression through my writing, speaking, and teaching.

Now, I understand that my life has a purpose; however, I almost didn't fulfill my life's potential due to momentary struggles. It's important to remember that life is about cumulative moments, which won't always be great. If I gave-up on my life, I would have cheated myself and numerous others who have benefited because of my decision, desire, and determination to fight for my life... and share my journey to recover from depression and a near suicide.

My path toward recovery might not be appropriate for others, but the purpose of my communication is for others to identify something that will help them. During challenging moments, it may feel as if there isn't anyone who cares or can help but understand that there's always someone who is willing to assist. The challenge (many times) is to be willing to identify assistance and give someone an opportunity to help.

Remember... no matter the length of your journey, don't forget to be your best!

The Day I Almost Committed Suicide

The American Foundation for Suicide Prevention (AFSP[4]) estimates that suicide is the tenth largest cause of death in the United States. Moreover, AFSP estimates that someone dies from suicide every 12.9 minutes... and I was almost part of these statistics.

The often-heard commentary after someone commits suicide is I didn't see that coming! or I never thought that *(insert name)* would do that. These thoughts are similar to the thoughts I've had after learning about someone's attempted or actual suicide. However, I never considered the possibility that anyone would think these thoughts about me, as suicide wasn't something I considered to be a possibility until it unexpectedly almost became my reality. My jolting and life-changing personal experiences is the reason that I'm compelled to share the details of my near-suicide to help others who might benefit (including anyone who feels similarly), those who attempt to help someone who has similar feelings, and others who don't understand the mindset of someone who is, was, or might be depressed or suicidal.

The day I almost committed suicide, I didn't plan it and it wasn't a thought that I had considered that day. This makes it intriguing that I almost took my life without any forethought. The best way that this experience can be described is that there was a system overload due to dealing with considerable mental and emotional stress over an extended period, which wasn't ever addressed or resolved.

---

[4] American Foundation for Suicide Prevention's website: afsp.org

The simplest way to describe this feeling is to relate it to someone who is physically exhausted and collapses. In this case, I was mentally and emotionally exhausted; moreover, I felt complete desperation and despair that my situation wouldn't improve.

I was mentally exhausted from constantly trying to do the right things and continually experiencing negative outcomes. These stressors were compounded as I also tried to battle the increasing severity of my untreated and unresolved depression. On this tragic day, my mind broke down: I no longer wanted to battle against so many unscrupulous individuals; I was tired of struggling with my depression; I thought that my life didn't have any value; I didn't want to fight for my life.

The morning of my mental health emergency, shortly after opening my eyes, I knew something wasn't normal. Usually, I get out of bed a few minutes after my eyes are open. On that day, I couldn't get out of my bed. I didn't want to do anything. I just stared ahead without any focus and almost in a trance. It felt as if a heavy fog entered my room, which prevented me from connecting in a logical way to realize that it was just a bad moment and not a reason to take my life.

Within an hour or so, I became very emotional after thinking about my failings, that I was a failure, that nobody wanted anything I had to offer, and that my future wasn't going to be any better. At this point, I started to consider ways to take my life. The more I thought about it, the more committed I became to taking my life; although, there was someone I still cared about... my mom.

As I finalized my approach to take my life, my desire to take the final step continued to grow. During my psychosis, I began to hear a rhythmical chant "Do it; do it; do it; ...; do it!" that became quicker and louder. I knew that this was the devil's voice because I had lost and surrendered my will to live. It was in these moments that I unexpectedly took action to save my life.

Despite my mental and emotional breakdown, I still cared about someone else... my mom. This is the only reason that with much reservation, I called one of my brothers to ensure that he would take care of our mom if I couldn't do it. My goal was to make a quick call and end it; instead, I started to breakdown. It was at this moment that my brother did something that was critical, he identified something was wrong and started to ask questions.

My brother wanted answers, but I didn't want to discuss anything with him; therefore, I ended the call. Then, my brother frantically kept calling back to reach me; however, I didn't want to talk to him or anyone else. As his calls kept coming, I eventually listened to his frantic messages and I halfheartedly returned his call, which led to the moment that changed everything.

During our conversation, my brother stressed that my current reality was only a moment and I needed to get past that moment. This message was important. Although, the comment that really resonated with me was after my brother said, "Use your own words to help yourself." (referring to my inspirational quotes). He also directed me to call our sister. The conversation with our sister was another important step to help me reconnect with reality.

Notwithstanding my sibling's heartfelt words and support, the thing that resonated with me the most was my brother's direction to "Use your own words to help yourself." This comment was powerful because it made me think about my work and its value. Also, my brother's comments made me consider the reasons I would write inspirational messages, but not believe them myself. These considerations jump-started the beginning of my journey to recover. Almost immediately, my thoughts began to change from irrational to evaluative, which made me think past the moments of my current situation to the possibility that my life did have value (even if I didn't understand my life's purpose).

Approximately three hours after I seriously considered suicide, I began to think about moving forward with my life. This was a significant change in my feelings and attitude from a little while earlier. Shortly thereafter, I went from desperation and despair to feeling that things could get better. Then, moment-by-moment, my desire and will to live strengthened.

The incredible and most significant step in my recovery is that approximately five hours after I almost committed suicide, my thoughts were directed toward others again. That evening, I was coincidentally scheduled and went to teach inmates about life management skills. Unfortunately, the jail wasn't open to volunteers that night. Nevertheless, by going to the jail that day, I unknowingly took critical steps toward my recovery. These forced steps helped to drive my life toward a greater appreciation, passion, and willingness to give-back (as we're all on a shared journey whether we realize it or not).

Life is about moments. Therefore, an individual's successes, failures, and life's value are defined by cumulative moments and not temporary setbacks during specific moments or related to perceived shortcomings. It won't always be easy to make forward-progress, but by making a choice to move forward a life can take unimaginable turns toward unexpected and unrealized happiness. However, during difficult times, individuals (like me) must be willing to share their feelings and struggles to have an opportunity to receive support.

Anyone who commits suicide ends their pain, but their life isn't the only loss. The other losses are to their family, friends, and anyone else who might have benefited from their contributions.

As for me in the months following my near-suicide, I have done things I never could have imagined, including blogging on The Huffington Post, becoming an advocate for understanding depression/mental health, and helping numerous individuals through sharing (publicly and privately) my journey to recover.

Nobody needs to struggle alone, as there's always someone who is willing to assist. The challenge (many times) is to be willing to identify assistance and give someone an opportunity to help.

Remember… no matter the length of your journey, don't forget to be your best!

Depression Can Be a Limiter: Willpower a Liberator

In a short period of time, someone's life can change from feelings of desperation, despair, and a belief that their life doesn't have any purpose to feeling renewed, purposeful, and committed to fighting for their dreams.

I know these feelings very well because on Tuesday, 3/18/14, I was moments from taking my life. The only thing that prevented me from doing so was a call I made to one of my brothers (out of concern about my mother's well-being). In making this phone call to ensure that my mother would be cared for if I was unable to do so, I allowed someone who cared and loved me to help me. Prior to this moment, I knew that I was loved by my family; although, my ego, concerns about being judged, and a false belief that strength means fighting your battles by yourself led me to needlessly suffer alone.

Since March, I've written and spoken extensively about my battle with depression and near-suicide to help others who have similar feelings. I never imagined or realized that being so open, vulnerable, and honest (the thing I was the most afraid to do) would be something that would save my life, help others, and hopefully change minds about depression.

It's been approximately nine months since I almost made a fateful decision to end my life. However, by fighting and willing myself to move forward, share my story, and not to give-up on myself or my dreams, my life has led to positive unexpected outcomes. Today, I'm a better, stronger, and a more positive man than I ever thought I could be simply because, I chose, fought, and was determined to make positive forward-progress.

A snapshot of my recovery:

- Shortly after my extremely depressive episode, I had very open, honest, and tearful conversations with my siblings, which allowed pent-up feelings to finally be released.

- About a month later, I wrote my book "Choosing To Take A Stand: Changed me, my life, and my destiny" to understand and release my painful experiences from the last few years. This soul wrenching was an extremely important step in my recovery, as it allowed me to finally address the things I couldn't discuss with anyone (including myself) for a very long time.

- In August, I shared my struggles with depression and my near-suicide with my Facebook family and friends. By disclosing this information, I released my fears about anyone learning about my personal challenges that I didn't want anyone to discover. This self-imposed fear about others' judgments about me was incorrectly given more value than my feelings and evaluations about myself.

- A week after my Facebook disclosure, I was a guest on the Maggie Linton Show (a national radio program). During my interview, I told my story. Then the unexpected happened, individuals who listened to my interview contacted me to share their battles with depression. This helped me realize that I wasn't alone, and my life did have value and purpose.

- In September, I accepted a great opportunity to blog on The Huffington Post. This experience has allowed me to share my story with a wider audience, educate others about depression and suicidal feelings, and hopefully prevent individuals from unnecessarily suffering alone or taking their life.

- Since September, I have transformed my life by continuing to help others by teaching inmates about life and business, being interviewed about my journey to overcome personal challenges, becoming a mentor for an at-risk teenager, and the thing that I'm proudest of is accepting an invitation to be the commencement speaker for the same school district that directed me to leave school in the tenth grade due to horrible academic performance.

Today, my life is still not as I want it to be, but its heading in the positive direction I want, and I'm living my life on purpose to give-back, inspire, educate, and uplift.

It's very hard to believe that I'm the same person (today) who gave-up on life, didn't feel I or my life had any value, and couldn't see any future for myself just nine months ago. I share my experiences very openly and honestly because I want to encourage anyone who feels that their life doesn't have value to not give-up on themselves or their dreams.

During my mental health challenges, my brother reminded me that life is about cumulative moments and not specific moments. He stressed to me that my feelings at that time were related to a moment, and I needed to get past it. These words helped me, and hopefully by sharing these words will help others, too.

My purpose and goals of sharing my story are to inspire others who believe that their life doesn't have value (and that things won't get any better) to keep moving forward.

A quote I wrote and use as my mantra to keep myself in a positive frame of mind:

> *Rain can only come down for so long so prepare for the sun to shine but act as if the sun is already out.*

Understand that letting someone know that you need assistance isn't a weakness; it's a strength to be able and willing to ask for help. Please don't needlessly suffer alone.

Nobody needs to struggle alone, as there's always someone who is willing to assist. The challenge (many times) is to be willing to identify assistance and give someone an opportunity to help.

I've chosen to step forward; I hope that you'll do the same.

Remember… no matter the length of your journey, don't forget to be your best!

Depression as a Mnemonic

Reference for anyone affected by depression:

- **(D)ecide** to seek treatment to obtain help to become better;

- **(E)ducate** yourself about depression by obtaining information and working with a medical professional;

- **(P)ersistence** is required to complete treatment(s), as it may take time and patience to resolve any medical issue(s);

- **(R)evaluate** any treatment plan(s) periodically for effectiveness and to ensure that it's the best for you;

- **(E)ncouragement** should be solicited from friends and family;

- **(S)eek** moments of silence to decompress, reflect, and relax on an ongoing basis;

- **(S)upport** others on their journey to get better, which can help you, too;

- **(I)nitiate** activities that can aid with stress relief and that can also create moments of happiness --- including laughter;

- **(O)pennesss** about mental health challenges can help to release stress instead of keeping it inside; releasing stress can also help to expedite the recovery process;

- **(N)ever Give-up**, as the feeling(s) of being depressed can be associated with a moment. Remember that life is about cumulative moments. Your next positive experiences are only moments away.

Nobody needs to struggle alone, as there's always someone who is willing to assist. The challenge (many times) is to be willing to identify assistance and give someone an opportunity to help.

Remember... no matter the length of your journey, don't forget to be your best!

Letter to Myself the Day Before My Near-Suicide: Written a Year Later

You're not going to believe this, but tomorrow your life will significantly change. By mid-morning, you'll make a life changing choice about whether you should live or die. During a few critical hours, you'll review your life, the things you've done, your current situation, and the things you want to do in the future. Based on these considerations, you will determine that you're a failure, no one wants anything you have to offer, and that you'll never be any better than you are today. You'll conclude that your life is worthless. Then, suddenly you'll make an emotional decision that you want to die. In the next few moments, you'll begin the initial steps to end your life.

During your preparation, you're going to make a final call. This call will be to one of your brothers, Johnnie. This call isn't to share your plans to end your life but instead to ensure that he'll take care of your mother if you couldn't do it. Your goal will be to convey strength during the call, obtain his commitment, and terminate the call as quickly as possible. However, the call will not go as planned. You will become emotional, your brother will ask if you're okay, and you will abruptly hang-up the phone. Then, your brother will frantically call back many times to try to reach you again.

In the next 45 minutes, you'll continue to plan your final moments. You'll be determined to not return your brother's calls. At this point, you'll have less than an hour before you end your life. Then, with reservations, you'll listen to your brother's messages before you reluctantly decide to return his calls. In the next few minutes, your brother will remind you that your current state is just a moment, which you need to get through to have a chance to survive. Your brother will also direct you to contact your sister (Joyce) to have a conversation.

After both conversations, your desire to end your life will not be as strong. You still haven't decided to save your life; although, your desire to end your life isn't as strong. Your thoughts will slowly change from desperation, defeat, and despair to a feeling that things could potentially get better.

Minute-by-minute and hour-by-hour you'll get stronger. You still aren't sure if you want to live, but you'll begin to consider things beyond this moment.

In a few hours, you'll muster the strength to get dressed. You'll also force yourself to go to a jail to teach inmates as scheduled. Unfortunately, you'll not be able to go inside because the jail is on lock-down. Nevertheless, by leaving the house and doing something meaningful, you've started to make progress.

A week and a day later, you'll give the most important presentation of your life; a presentation about belief[5] at a Healthy Living Series event. Somehow, you'll force yourself to pretend that you're happy. At the end of this presentation, you'll jump around and dance as if you don't have a care in the world. After this presentation, you and your cameraman will discuss that something was different about this

---

[5] Reference Appendix C: The Presentation That Changed and Saved My Life for details about the presentation "Belief: A Powerful Component of Success", along with a link to it.

presentation. Suddenly, you'll realize that you were standing in front of an audience while trying to convince yourself to believe in life, yourself, and your future.

In about two months, you'll write a book entitled "Choosing To Take A Stand: Changed me, my life, my destiny." This book will chronicle your battle with depression and the reasons that you almost committed suicide, along with recommendations for recovery. Writing this book will allow you to process many of the issues that you never fully addressed. This writing experience will expedite your healing, self-awareness, and your determination to fight for your life.

In about five months, you'll see a Facebook posting that will question the reason(s) that Robin Williams committed suicide. In response to this post, you'll share your battle with depression and journey away from a near-suicide a few months prior with family and friends on Facebook. After this public disclosure, you'll go even further to share your story to help others during an interview on the Maggie Linton Show.

In about six months, you'll begin to write about depression and suicidal thoughts in a very meaningful and humanizing way. Shortly thereafter you'll read an article on The Huffington Post's website soliciting individuals to share their journey with depression. You'll use this opportunity to share your blog posts about your own mental health challenges. Then, you'll receive a surprising offer to become a blogger on The Huffington Post.

In about eight months, you'll begin to write more frequently about depression to raise awareness, understanding, and compassion. Around the same time, while seeking to speak to college students about depression, you'll connect (by chance) with a college's Dream-Catchers' program administrator, which will result in you becoming a mentor. You'll then be matched with an intelligent young man with similar challenges to those in your past, which will create an immediate bond between the two of you. Furthermore, based on your experiences overcoming numerous educational challenges and involvement with Dream-Catchers, you'll be asked to be the commencement speaker for the same school district from which you were directed to leave high school in the tenth grade after failing 6 of 7 classes and graduating in the bottom 8%.

Around the ninth month, you'll feel reborn. At this point, you'll not recognize the person who will want to commit suicide tomorrow.

In the tenth and eleventh months prior to the first anniversary of your awakening after a near-suicide, you'll be asked to be an alumni panelist at the university that you had to take non-degree classes to prove your ability to perform college-level work before being admitted. You'll also be asked to be the keynote speaker for a Black History Month celebration at the college that you left many years earlier due to academic performance issues (including two semesters with a 0.00 average).

During these worst moments of your life and with minimal resources, you'll give all of yourself to help others. You'll learn that happiness isn't as you had imagined and expected it to be. You'll finally realize that your happiness comes from within and while helping others to thrive. As you work to rebuild your life, you'll no longer navigate life by happenstance. Instead, you'll design and develop your life on purpose; the way you want it to be. You'll create a life of service that's focused on educating, inspiring, and uplifting others.

These are the things that can happen if you choose to get past a difficult moment tomorrow. If you do, you'll have an incredible year as an advocate for depression, suicide prevention, workplace bullying, ethics, and more. These accomplishments aren't actions of someone who is desperate, defeated, or in despair. However, if you choose to commit suicide tomorrow, then you'll not have a voice or a chance to positively impact lives (including your own).

Now, that you're aware of these positive changes in your near future… if you allow yourself to get past these difficult moments: Will you make an impulsive choice to end your life tomorrow? If you do, you'll not have an opportunity to share your story (e.g., blogging, interviews, speaking engagements) with hundreds of individuals who might save themselves or someone else because of your decision to fight for your life. You need to understand that if you choose to save your life tomorrow, your decision will not only impact you. Your choice will also positively affect many others who will benefit from your work over the next year and beyond.

So, tomorrow, please don't make a momentary and emotional decision that will prevent you from doing all the things described herein while also preventing yourself from achieving your potential to do things that you can't even imagine yet. If you commit suicide, you'll end your pain, but you'll also cause others to suffer because you needlessly forgot that you're loved. By choosing to live, you'll have opportunities to positively impact, inspire, and change lives.

Your brother, Johnnie, will tell you tomorrow, Stacey, this is just a moment; you need to get past this moment.

<u>To my brother Johnnie, my sister Joyce, and the countless others who provided their support over the past year:</u>

Thank you for recognizing and supporting me during my mental health crisis. Your ability to help me carefully navigate through these critical moments is very much appreciated, along with your love and support as I continue to heal, become stronger, and develop into the man I never imagined I could ever possibly be.

Depression: My Journey Through the Fog

My perspective on life has almost always been 'the glass is half full' (even during difficult moments). Therefore, I never thought that depression would be something that might affect me. My limited understanding about depression was that someone felt bad or sad; however, I never really thought about the personal impact of depression. My lack of knowledge about depression (its symptoms, effects, impacts, and treatment options) would later prove to be troublesome for me.

Depression is a personal experience that impacts individuals differently; although, understanding the way depression can impact someone's attitude, behavior, emotions, and outlook are important to help anyone affected or effected by this mental health challenge. The evolution of my depression might not be the same as others, but it's still important to share my experiences so that others can benefit and hopefully choose to seek treatment before their depression advances.

<u>My depression advanced in phases:</u>

- <u>Early Warning</u> – Emotional reactions start to happen periodically; there aren't any continuous periods of feeling bad.

- <u>Early Onset</u> – An increased awareness that something doesn't feel normal. There's a heightened recognition that the periods of feeling bad or down are more frequent. These feelings mark the initial signs that emotional and mental changes have started to impact daily activities.

- Noticeable Impact – Feelings of being down or not wanting to participate in normal activities start to increase. There's a decreased desire to be productive, engage with others, or continue activities normally used for relaxation and stress relief. Negative thoughts about life and the future start to happen more often.

- Disengagement – Time spent on productive activities and with others occurs less frequently. There are increased instances of feeling negative about life, more time spent alone, and more frequent excuses to not be around others.

- Disruption - Bad days start to be the norm and good days seem to occur less frequently. There are increasing emotional periods and outbursts, which impact positive thoughts, productivity, and led to increased periods of self-imposed isolation. Plans aren't really considered anymore. Thoughts become focused on ways to end the pain and suffering.

- Life Impacting – Thoughts are usually very negative about others generally and life specifically; periods of isolation are normal. Emotional outbursts/reactions increase, normal activities are almost non-existent, suicidal thoughts change from thoughts to fantasies / plans, and the desire to live no longer exists.

If any of these phases are identified in yourself or others, it's time to take steps to begin:

- Recovery – Actions taken to resolve any emotional or mental health challenges that affect positive thinking: attitude, behavior, emotions, and outlook. Efforts to actively manage negative thoughts begin, which help to increase positive feelings, productivity gains, personal happiness, and future plans. Previously discontinued activities slowly start to return to normal.

This description about the way my mental health challenges evolved is a personal perspective about the potential impacts of depression. This information shouldn't be used as a medical reference.

Notwithstanding, anybody who experiences feelings of depression should seek assistance as soon as possible to minimize any potential negative impacts.

Anyone affected by depression should understand that there are many different options that can be used to treat and resolve mental health challenges; for example, exercise, discussions with family/friends, massage therapy, medicine, meditation, prayer, psychologist/psychiatrist, support groups, writing, and more.

A couple of my past articles[6] can be used to help someone who might be depressed, along with ways individuals can help themselves.

Nobody needs to struggle alone, as there's always someone who is willing to assist. The challenge (many times) is to be willing to identify assistance and give someone an opportunity to help.

---

[6] Reference the articles "Helping Someone Who Might Be Depressed" and "Depression as a Mnemonic".

Remember… no matter the length of your journey, don't forget to be your best!

Someone Stopped and Listened; It's the Only Reason I'm Still Alive

July is Minority Mental Health Awareness Month, which is dedicated to raising awareness about mental health challenges, especially in underserved and underrepresented communities. Therefore, as a person of color, I feel compelled to share my journey to help save lives, as I've battled depression for years and was almost another suicide statistic.

Since disclosing my mental health crisis about me being moments from taking my life in March 2014, I've had numerous conversations with family and friends about the reasons that someone like me (who by all outward appearances seems to be happy and positive) could or would take my life. These types of evaluative considerations are the reasons that too many individuals miss the warning signs that someone is having a mental health emergency that requires medical attention.

Depression isn't something I knew about as an adolescent, considered, or thought would ever happen to me; although, once it emerged, I clearly understood its effects, even if I didn't know its formal name. My limited knowledge about depression (until it happened to me) highlights the importance and significance of teaching mental health education during a youth's developmental years.

At the time of my near-suicide, I didn't plan it, even though I was under considerable stress due to a multitude of life's circumstances. The amazing reality about my experiences that potentially fateful day is the sudden dissent into feelings of disillusionment, desperation, defeat, and despair.

Shortly after opening my eyes, I immediately knew that something didn't feel normal. I couldn't focus, didn't have a desire to get out of bed, and a heavy fog encompassed my room. Then, moment-by-moment, my desire and commitment to take my life solidified. In the final stage of my planning, I was very and uncontrollably emotional because I didn't want to take my life, but I had assessed, realized, and projected the lack of my value on many different levels (e.g., personally, professionally, spiritually).

Notwithstanding my commitment to take my life that day, there was only one thing left that I cared about and needed to ensure was taken care of to be free to take the final action, which was my mother. This is the only reason that I made a call to a relative, which took everything in my being to do given my mental frailty. It took several aborted attempts to complete the call to my next oldest brother to ensure that if anything happened to me that our mother would be okay, since I'm her primary caregiver.

My planned final call didn't go as expected because I became even more emotional during our conversation, as I could no longer contain my emotions. Immediately, my brother asked if I was alright. However, I didn't want to tell him anything or talk anymore. Then, without any warning, I hung-up the phone. This abrupt end to our conversation made my brother realize that something was seriously wrong. He kept calling back in a frantic attempt to reach me. After numerous calls and messages, I finally and reluctantly returned his call. This was the beginning of things starting to turn-around, along with me beginning to fight for my life, faith, and desire to live.

Once I decided to return my brother's calls, he slowly but

surely redirected my thoughts from that of worthlessness toward a focus on that moment only. My brother stressed and convinced me that my mental health emergency was a moment that I needed to get past. He also encouraged me to contact our sister to discuss my feelings and the situation that led to me wanting to take my life, which I did with lots of reservations. These conversations are the only reasons that my life was saved that day.

The hardest thing that I did over the past year is to boldly document my story, along with my path toward recovery. By finally releasing the feelings, emotions, and situations that led to my desire to want to take my life... I started to begin a process of healing. As an educator (even though I never wanted to share my very personal story), I understand the extreme importance of sharing difficult life's lessons to help and inspire others, especially for a taboo topic that many don't understand, aren't comfortable discussing, or associate and direct negative stigmas toward anyone who experiences any mental health challenges.

Depression is a medical condition which affects the body. Anyone affected by it should seek treatment, as it would be done for any other bodily ailments. No one should feel inferior due to identifying a bona fide medical condition. Moreover, it's far past time to stop classifying depression as something that happens to the weak, the crazy, or any other judgmental comments. Mental health challenges aren't the issue; the real issues are the unnecessary judgments that impact anyone's willingness to ask for or get help. Mental health is bodily health! If someone has any health issues that affect their well-being, then help should be sought without any thoughts about others' considerations related to their strength of mind, body, or character. Stop judging; start helping; save lives!

The outcome wasn't the same for a mother (Mary Hanson) who contacted me early this year after reading one of my articles Letter to Myself the Day Before My Near-Suicide: Written a Year Later[7] about my battle with depression.

Mrs. Hanson shared with me a story about a phone call she had with her son (Brian Hanson) that was in some ways similar to the one I had with my brother. During their phone call, Brian told her that something didn't feel right; however, he couldn't describe or identify the words to detail his feelings.

Early the next morning, Mrs. Hanson was awakened by a knock on her door that she'll never forget. She was told by police officers that her son (who a few hours earlier told her that he wasn't feeling normal) took his life. This mother would then bury her son approximately a week later on his birthday instead of celebrating it.

This fateful story and mine are compelling reasons that if someone expresses concerns that something isn't or doesn't feel right with them, please stop and pay attention… as this might be the last opportunity to save their life. After reading this article, beyond reflecting, sharing, and commenting, please make a commitment to yourself and others that if anyone communicates something similar to you that… #Iwillstopandlisten.

---

[7] Reference the article "Letter to Myself the Day Before My Near-Suicide Written a Year Later".

July is dedicated to minority mental health awareness; however, discussions about mental health should be a yearlong conversation regardless of race.

I sincerely hope that by sharing my extremely personal story that it will help, change, and save lives. There shouldn't be any shame directed toward anyone who experiences a mental health challenge; although, there is something wrong with any society that directs unnecessary judgments about someone's mental, physical, or emotional health that prevents anyone from seeking and getting treatment that could save their life.

Depression Can Lead to Individuals Questioning Their Value(s)

Value (whether it's personal, family, financial, moral, or spiritual) is pursued by everyone. It can be a driving force, an artificial projection, or sometimes used as a weapon to diminish, demoralize, or devalue someone's contributions. Notwithstanding, the issue with assessing value is that it's an artificial evaluation of worth based on an assessor's assumptions, which doesn't always reflect intrinsic or extrinsic value.

Depression can have various sources[8], such as psychological (irregular brain activity), physiological (a chemical imbalance), situational (a specific event), or periodic (certain time periods). As a result, it can sometimes be difficult to identify, treat, or resolve depression, unless the source is identified. Moreover, the willingness to seek treatment can be adversely impacted due to inappropriate projections about someone's personal strength or mental fortitude by improperly associating negative terms to an individual's bona fide medical condition, such as labeling someone as weak or crazy, respectively.

Individuals affected by certain types of depression tend to question their value. Oftentimes because of external forces that put into question their worth due to bullying, culture, comparative value, meanness, or someone's amusement. There are also internal negative factors that affect someone's valuations, which can be amplified by ongoing personal attacks, situational factors, or internal considerations that lead

---

[8] Reference the article "Functioning While Depressed".

to a breaking point for pent-up struggles.

If you asked someone who almost took their life, "Are you glad to still be alive?" Numerous individuals will respond in the affirmative. Unfortunately, too many times, individuals are lost not because there was a desire to die, but instead there was an urgent need for the pain to end... right now!

Can you imagine living a life that the days are always dark from the inside out, your situation isn't getting any better, and there isn't any hope that things will change? Even if you can't, you can surmise that this wouldn't be a pleasant feeling. Now consider the additional stress of wanting to share your feelings, but are worried about being evaluated, judged, chastised, called names, or worse during your most challenging times. These are some of the reasons that individuals affected by depression suffer alone, don't share their feelings, and sometimes sadly choose to have an untimely ending.

For me, my depression caused me to question my value, along with feelings of disillusionment, desperation, defeat, and despair. However, it also led to an unexpected discovery that I wouldn't be forced into submission by not being true to myself by being culpable to unethical/questionable behavior or being bullied by senior executives without any means to properly protect myself[9] from these unprovoked, unwanted, and unnecessary attacks.

During the worst period in my life, I pushed myself to

---

[9] Reference this article in Appendix A: Laws Protect Certain Classes from Workplace Abuse: Why Not Everyone?

continue to make forward-progress to explore different opportunities, which led me to discover my true passions that I might not have ever discovered. Steven Pressfield might have described my period of enlightenment the best on an episode[10] of *Super Soul Sunday* with Oprah Winfrey. During this show, he described resistance as a negative force that occurs on the way to self-fulfillment. He also said that the closer someone gets to the achievement of their goals, the more resistance that will be experienced.

My transformation began at the beginning of my dissent into a deep depression in April 2012. At first, I withdrew, didn't want to do anything, or talk to anyone. Then, I had an overwhelming and unexpected urge to write. Writing was something that I previously considered; although, these early feelings weren't as strong. All I knew was that I had to write; it was something that consumed my soul.

In May 2013 at the onset of my writing journey, I didn't have a plan, but my inner voice drove me to write. Writing became and still is one of my biggest comforts. Without it, I might not have made it past the months following my near-suicide. The most important thing I did during this challenging period was to release my pain to prevent from doing anything that would lead to self-destructive behavior.

Writing led me to redefine my personal values. The more I wrote, the more others identified with my journey and the stories I shared about humanity. After working with at-risk young men (some of them inmates), I realized that most of the things I did, enjoyed, and was passionate about were related

---

[10] Recording of Mr. Pressfield's comments: youtube.com/watch?v=hHsvipp8rjs

to teaching and helping others.

During my self-discovery to recapture my desire to live a fulfilled life, I remembered a Happy News Telegram received from my first-grade teacher (Mrs. Powell) who wrote "Stacey is my right arm! He helps everyone and is an inspiration to those children not as gifted." If my mother didn't keep this note, then it might have been lost, along with a missed opportunity to help identify my life's passion and purpose. Thankfully it wasn't lost because after reading this note, I realized that I've always been a teacher; teaching is something that I'm passionate about and driven to do. These days, my teaching manifests itself through my writing, speaking engagements, teaching in college classrooms/jails, and mentoring.

While others tried to diminish, demoralize, or devalue me personally, along with trying to have me behave in ways that are inconsistent with my morals and values. I affirmed my value(s), which in-turn allowed me to redefine the meaning of happiness for me. I used to believe that happiness is tied to monetary gains, rising to executive levels, and hanging-out with so-called friends. Now, I understand that my value isn't related to any of these things; instead, it's simply driven by my commitment to unconditionally be the individual that I want to be, my ability to help others, and knowing that my contributions have helped or led to someone having a better life.

Over the last few years, I lost a lot of financial value, material things, and in so many ways reductions in my self-esteem; however, I didn't lose myself, my values, or my commitment to try to do the right things not just for me but also society.

Depression is a disease that isn't always understood, can have debilitating effects, and is sometimes a preventable silent killer. Although, depression does have a benefit in that it can help to identify that something is wrong. This discovery could be related to something psychological, physiological, situational, or periodic. Although, for me, depression was the catalyst to recognize that I wasn't in environments, situations, or circumstances which allowed me to live my best and fulfilled life.

Difficult times can cause individuals to surrender to the pressure by withdrawing, acting inappropriately toward others, or to engaging in personally destructive behavior (e.g., alcoholism, drug addiction). Notwithstanding these possibilities, depression can also drive actions for individuals to determine the source(s) of issues to develop a strategy to identify, manage, and resolve anything that might negatively impact someone's life.

The most valuable lesson I've learned from my battle with depression and recovery after a near-suicide is that any unexplained changes (sudden or not) in someone's behavior(s) should be examined. At times, individuals who experience a personal storm might not recognize the warning signs to take action(s) for themselves; therefore, others should make a commitment to keep a watchful eye for any changes in someone's behavior(s) that appear to be atypical. The worst thing that can happen and sometimes the biggest regret(s) are from individuals who noticed something that appeared to be uncharacteristic and dismissed their concerns about these changes as being just a phase.

Please don't let your thoughts after someone's dissent into

destructive behavior or an untimely demise be... I knew something didn't seem or appear to be right with them. I wish I had given it more consideration, had a conversation, or simply asked a question that might have saved their life.

Journey After a Near-Suicide to Educate, Remove Stigmas, and Save Lives

After learning about Robin Williams' death (8/11/14), I paused, reflected, and privately understood the types of demons that might have affected him. This would have been the end of my thoughts about it after a few days; however, there was an insensitive Facebook post that same day which made a judgmental comment about the reasons that anyone would commit suicide. This comment bothered me, and it drove me to do something I wasn't ready but was compelled to do.

On 8/12/14, I wrote a Facebook post that began an unexpected writing journey about depression over the past year. In this post, I boldly shared my battle with depression and journey to recover after a near-suicide in March 2014. Releasing this post was one of the most heart-wrenching decisions I've made in my life. Nonetheless, it was the moment that I started to live (again). Almost immediately, I felt better because I released feelings that I had anguished, worried, and was embarrassed about that were barriers to my recovery.

On 8/18/14, I appeared on the Maggie Linton Show to share my story[11] with a national audience. At first, discussing my journey was easier than I expected, but about halfway through this interview I choked-up and struggled to continue. Fortunately, I was able to finish sharing my story. After my interview, I said, I wish I hadn't gotten emotional, and Mrs. Linton replied, "That's what made it real."

---

[11] Watch this video at: youtu.be/dUi2IQxcHrM

It's interesting that I had such reservations about discussing my story, because within a couple months of my near-suicide I documented my raw feelings and emotions in my memoir. My goal in writing this book was to help others affected by depression (directly or indirectly). Although, the feedback received, questions asked, and personal battles shared made me realize that there were many individuals who didn't understand depression beyond knowing that it made someone feel bad or sad.

I never imagined that my articles would affect so many. I received private messages from family/friends, classmates from high school, and strangers who shared their journeys with me. Each of these by itself was very powerful, but the messages that touched me the most were from family members and friends who contacted this stranger to tell me about the story of their loved one lost to this disease. These individuals told me that my articles helped them to understand the way their loved one might have felt in their final moments, something that person did before their death, or the most meaningful comments to me were that my articles helped to answer a question that was previously unresolved.

As for me, I'd love to write that this is a fairytale ending to my year-long writing project, but it isn't. I still battle depression due to some life circumstances and have some moments that feel like bottomless lows. Notwithstanding these feelings, I have learned ways to better manage periods of depression, understand ways to release my pain(s), and most importantly I use my support system, which was always available. However, I limited my options for recovery due to my false assumptions that I would be negatively judged versus being helped.

This piece marks my (planned) final article about depression and my battle with it. I truly hope that my materials will be shared to let others know that they're not alone.

As I wrote in my first HuffPost blog entry Depression – An Unnecessary Stigma[12] (disclosure about my depression because of Robin Williams' death-by-suicide):

> Remember, from the day we're born until the day we're buried, we don't do anything alone. Therefore, don't be afraid to disclose your struggles and ask for help. Being vulnerable to share your challenges isn't a weakness, but instead a strength. The challenge many times is convincing yourself otherwise.

Individuals must take care of their mental health along with their physical well-being. Please don't learn the hard way like I did; act now to save your life because I'm sure someone is more than willing to say #Iwillstopandlisten.

Best wishes on your journey and always remember to… Be your best!

---

[12] Reference the article "Depression – An Unnecessary Stigma".

What If?!

What if a decision you were afraid to, chose not to, or didn't make could've changed your life and others? This might seem to be an unanswerable question but consider another. What if you didn't act, decide, or respond because you allowed someone's considerations to stop you from doing the right thing or pursing your dream(s); were directed away from doing something that might help you to achieve your potential; caused you to doubt yourself due to their questions about your abilities or capabilities? These types of reflective questions can lead individuals to later think... What if?!

What If?! is a question asked by many throughout their lives, but the worst time to consider it is on your deathbed. Too many people don't achieve their potential simply due to fear (e.g., taking a chance/step, others' opinions, failing). A video[13] entitled "Live Your Life Over" about individuals not living up to their potential captures this best, along with adding that dreams sometimes die forever because the individual who could have given them life didn't pursue them.

In Jim Carey's commencement address at the 2014 Maharishi University of Management's graduation, he shared that his father didn't believe it was possible for him to be a successful comedian... so he didn't pursue it. Instead, he accepted a safe job as an accountant, but was let go from this job; subsequently, his family struggled to survive. During this

---

[13] Watch the "Motivational Video – Live Your Life Over" at: youtu.be/jFunNbeIzRk

speech[14] Mr. Carey said, "So many of us choose our paths out of fear disguised as practicality." He went on to say, "I learned many great lessons from my father. Not the least of which is that you can fail at what you don't want, so you might as well take a chance at doing what you love."

What if?! the direction of your life or your life's purpose wasn't driven by the decisions that you made, but instead by the ones you tormented over and didn't make? Could these moments of indecision (if addressed directly) have been the catalyst that pushed you toward a direction that otherwise you might not have gone? These tough moments or questions might be presented as a crossroad to determine if someone is ready to live a life that wasn't or couldn't be imagined as a possibility.

These types of internal dilemmas and conflicts I know very well. During difficult and critical moments in my life, I questioned my beliefs to determine if the things I said and did were "really" true to me. At times, someone will proclaim to have strong beliefs about something until the person is able to make a choice or decision. Then, once confronted or forced to make a choice, these same individuals will back away from, question, or attack their own position.

During challenging years, I made difficult choices due to conflicts between my beliefs and my willingness to be complicit to others' unethical activities. These gut-wrenching choices led to unimaginable tough times that had me within moments of taking my life, but at the same time these visceral

---

[14] Listen to Mr. Carey's comments during his commencement address from 10:10 – 11:46: youtu.be/V80-gPkpH6M?t=610

moments caused me to grow the most emotionally, mentally, and spiritually. Moreover, I learned that my choices reflect my commitment to who I am and who I want to be, but are also driven by my desire to not want to later ask myself:

> What if I hadn't done the right thing and chose to ignore or went along with questionable, unethical, or illegal activities for the sake of maintaining my job and financial standing by sacrificing my principles?

"By Choosing To Take A Stand" against actions and behaviors I knew weren't right, I began to redefine and transform myself into unexpectedly the better man I am today. These types of tough moments (for example: failure, disappointment, and loss) are sometimes the biggest factors and impetus for growth and enlightenment. I could have played it safe (like Jim Carey's father) and made a very good salary for myself, but I wouldn't have been true to myself, my beliefs, or also self-fulfilled. The amazing thing that happened during my darkest days was that I really got to learn about who I am, which I didn't do before… and maybe in some ways was afraid to do it. Today I can honestly and confidently look at myself in the mirror and say, "I know who I am!", which is a priceless feeling.

Frederick Nietzsche's quote, "He who has a why to live can bear almost any how" has significant meaning for my life. If it wasn't for my ability to determine my "why" during the tumultuous years, I wouldn't have been able to handle my "how". This would have also prevented me from discovering my passion, purpose, and ability to maximize my personal value, which is simply to help and teach others.

> Note: By addressing my life's challenges directly, I unleashed and gave myself permission to: create an educational non-profit that teaches inmates about life, business, and soft skills; become an inspirational speaker who discusses overcoming challenges; helped depressed individuals and those who lost loved ones to death-by-suicide to better understand this mental health challenge, educated individuals about workplace bullying; connected with thousands around the world through my writing; learned to live my life on purpose.

The easiest thing to do during tough times is to have a negative perspective, engage in destructive behavior, or sometimes just quit trying. However, this type of defeatist attitude won't help you to do something that matters for yourself and others. While confronted with difficult choices that have a potential to effect my future (and sometimes others), I found solace in one of my quotes from my "It's a Crazy World… Learn From It" series: Many individuals are afraid of jail; however, individuals often lock themselves in their own prisons. Be your own warden and set yourself free of unnecessary worry, doubts, and limitations.

The tough lessons I've learned is that beliefs[15] aren't always as firm as some might think. Too often, individuals proclaim to have a belief (something generally believed to be true), but many times it's simply a consideration (something true for that person) that might change under certain criteria. Although, many actions are based on convenience (exceptions depending on circumstances), instead of a

---
[15] Reference this article in Appendix B: Belief: An Underutilized Tool.

personal belief[16] or consideration.

Individuals can miss opportunities because there isn't a belief that something is possible, their considerations aren't enough to drive their desire(s)/determination to act, or it isn't convenient for someone to persevere to summon their internal strength to move forward despite (sometimes overwhelming) obstacles.

There are so many What if?! questions that go unanswered due to fear but imagine the potential impact of pushing yourself to make a tough choice that could positively change your life or others. Might your actions or behavior be different during challenging moments? Perhaps... Unfortunately, unless individuals make active choices to What if?! questions, the outcome of these missed opportunities or decisions might not ever be known.

Instead of wondering right now... What if the writer of the piece is correct?... create a list of What if?! questions for yourself and answer them. By actively choosing and proactively planning to make decisions about your life, you'll never have to wonder... What if?!

---

[16] Recording of the presentation Belief: A Powerful Component of Success is available: slyoung.com/power-of-belief

It's Still a Wonderful Life

Every year in December I look forward to watching some if not all of the movie "It's a Wonderful Life". I never realized the reason that I enjoyed this movie so much. Of course, it's a holiday movie with a great turnaround story and a wonderful message, but there are a lot of movies with similar messages. Yet, there's something that I connected with in this movie that I just couldn't stop thinking about at all.

Then, as I prepared to write this piece, I got it! It's the critical elements of this movie: a man working hard to fulfill his dream, making the tough choice between staying for family reasons or following dreams, dealing with organizational / workplace bullies, being negatively impacted by unethical individuals, affected by the negative consequences, contemplating deciding to die-by-suicide, desiring to live again after self-reflection, remembering that others are available to help, and realizing that everyone's life matters.

In 2006, I left an excellent corporate job after almost five years to pursue other opportunities. The timing was perfect to make a change because the company offered buyouts to reduce staff after the merger's completion. As a result, I wanted to explore my career options; although, my considerations remained local due to caring for an elderly parent for whom I didn't want to make any significant location changes.

Over the next few years, I worked with organizations and individuals who were determined to 'win at any cost'. I witnessed everything from nepotism, contractor abuse, malfeasance (manipulating audit reports/committing fraud to onboard severely underutilized contracted government resources), hostile work environments/workplace bullying), and more. My options were to become complicit by 'going-along-to-get-along' or to refuse to be a party to unethical actions. The stress of continually having to decide between protecting my income stream or removing myself from environments with unsavory individuals was mentally and physically exhausting.

The easiest thing to do was to behave as others did, but it wouldn't have allowed me to be who I wanted to be or to do the things I was driven to do. The challenge is that being under the power of individuals who have direct or indirect power over you can be taxing and sometimes can cause individuals to buckle under the pressure to comply (willingly, unwillingly). Consequently, individuals who make these character and sometimes life changing choices are directed away from the person that they might otherwise be. For me, this wasn't an option because I still had control over my choices and wasn't going to be unduly influenced to do something I didn't consciously choose.

Tough choices can lead to difficult moments, but at the same time can also help to develop character and transform ordinary lives into extraordinary experiences. This doesn't mean that someone will be financially well-off because some of the greatest moments of happiness don't have anything to do with money. It has more to do with: who you are, the things you do, who you help, the positive changes you make, and the things you leave behind after your life is over for others to benefit.

The thing that I've learned is that… It's better to be broke and in love with yourself, than rich and not know yourself.

During my period of severe depression caused by dealing with the negative consequences of refusing to be unethical or bullied (including attempts to manipulate me to do unethical things), I began to dissect every portion of my life to ask (repeatedly)… What's wrong with me?!?! This reflective question is asked by someone who is or is about to be defeated, dejected, depressed, and potentially delusional. This is also an example of the kind of projections brought about by individuals who recklessly do bad things (some purposely) to others.

These types of impactful feelings and considerations aren't always related to someone's personal strength or mental fortitude; instead, it has everything to do with the effects of confronting life altering choices directly. Moreover, it leads to questions about whether someone will allow abusive, manipulative, or purposeful negative actions to go unchallenged or silently suffer alone. Either way, these types of things can have a devastating effect on someone's perspective, psyche, and purpose.

I know these affects all too well as after I opened my eyes in March 2014; I was a beaten, battered, and a broken man. I didn't plan it; I wasn't ready for it; however, I was done with life and wanted the pain to be over. As I made my planned final call to my brother to ensure that my mom would be cared for after I was gone. I started to reconnect (during my psychosis) with my own reality that I mattered, and my life still had value, even if I wasn't fully connected with the thought at that time.

During moments of deep self-reflection, the negative parts of our lives can be amplified to extreme levels. There can be a blockage that prevents someone from remembering that today isn't yesterday; today is a new day and by taking a step, things can have a greater potential to change toward the positive. The future isn't defined; therefore, there are plenty of opportunities to reshape and redefine the next phase of our lives to redirect toward a different journey.

I made this choice on the same day I almost died-by-suicide. There was something that my brother, sister, and a good friend said that day that brought me closer to reality. The thing that echoed in my mind (over and over) was my brother's message that directed me to think beyond the current moment. The nice thing about life is that it's about cumulative moments. If you don't like the current one, then do something about it because the next moment is just a heartbeat away.

I didn't like the path I was heading, so even during my deepest depression and the most difficult years I took steps to change my life. I wrote, learned about myself, discovered the sources of my happiness, and started to build a new career, which has allowed me to help thousands of individuals that I otherwise wouldn't have encountered without actively dealing with the sources of my pain. Heartache and frustration are parts of the human experience and none of us will navigate life without experiencing them. The tricks are to: deal with the things that create pain as quickly as possible, don't be afraid to be vulnerable to share your struggles, and explore various options or opportunities to discover ways to feel, do, and be better.

During my darkest days on my way toward recovery, I learned to appreciate and celebrate the small successes, but also, I decided to not beat-up myself over things that are outside of my control. Bad moments can either make you bitter or better; it's a choice. If you're made to feel bitter, then it will take a lot longer to feel better. Bitterness is something that's usually controllable; therefore, if you're going to use your energy then you should use it for the positive to work on being better.

As I work to rebuild and redefine my life on purpose, it's not in the place I want it to be yet; however, I'm committed to working every day to build the life I want on purpose. The most important lesson during my journey is that life won't ever be perfect and that you don't have to be at your best to make a difference for yourself and others. Don't wait for a perfect time to create your turnaround; actively work on it every day, especially and mindfully during your worst days. Over the last few years, I lost so much financially and almost lost myself and my life. Notwithstanding, I've used my pain to write and communicate extensively about dealing with sometimes taboo topics and issues to help myself and others to do and be better.

It took many years for me to learn that happiness originates on the inside and has nothing to do with material possessions. The most valuable gift of life is time; therefore, I choose wisely the way it's used, allocated to others, and maximized. By being true to myself (during good and bad times) I don't ever have to wonder who I am or if I'm doing the right things for me. The trouble many times is unnecessarily changing ourselves to please others, which if we're not careful will lead us to a place we don't necessarily want to be.

Perspective is one of the greatest gifts of living a fulfilled life. If you don't like your current one, look for ways to change it. It's the only way to ensure that you increase the possibilities of saying during good and bad times… it's still a wonderful life!

High School Friends; Different Ethical Paths; Almost Identical Tragic Endings

This month (March) is National Ethics Awareness Month, which represents an additional opportunity to focus on and discuss ethical behavior. This topic is especially important to me as someone who took a stand against unethical behavior in several organizations (even though my ethical behavior unbelievably led to inconceivable personal costs). Regardless of the anguish experienced, I would do the same things again today. My strong belief is that a choice to remain silent about or be complicit to wrongdoings (regardless of the potential consequences) is never an acceptable option.

The following characterizes the impact of ethical choices (good and bad) on the lives of two high school friends that led to considerable turmoil for both of their lives. One would be dead months after being terminated by their employer after alleged discrepancies in expense reimbursement requests were discovered. In public records, the company terminating their employment communicated that the expenses weren't properly reimbursable or were reimbursements requested that were more than the amounts spent. The other individual would be moments from death-by-suicide after being negatively impacted due to making several difficult choices to not participate or be complicit to unethical behavior (including workplace bullying). These experiences are shared to highlight the issues, impacts, and devastation that can result for anyone who faces or confronts ethical dilemmas, which were created by themselves or forced upon them by others.

During high school these friends had a lot of good times

together but were on different paths. One excelled and was academically inclined; the other was mischievous and not academically focused. Even though they took different educational and career paths, both had ambitious dreams. A while after high school, these friends didn't reconnect until a coincidental meeting at a university. At this point, one friend was driven to become a corporate mogul while the other struggled to connect with their academic pursuits. Regardless of these differences, both of their academic and professional ambitions drove them to achieve future successes.

Years later their paths crossed again. Up until this time, both achieved numerous academic, professional, and personal successes; although, their lives and pursuits continued to be vastly different. One of them achieved the prestige of becoming a financial broker and living a flashy New York lifestyle of the rich and famous, which many individuals desire. The other one struggled to rebuild their life after voluntarily leaving successful careers in organizations that had cultures, values, and authority figures who were unethical and desired to win at any cost. These beliefs and highly questionable efforts to achieve success didn't align with their concepts of ethical behavior or decent treatment of people.

Ethics is something that's stressed throughout people's lives by their families/friends, churches, schools, organizations, and employers. It's something that's communicated as being responsible and valuable; however, the personal and sometimes professional costs to achieve and maintain ethical standards aren't always considered worth it. It's this kind of carefree mentality that results in too many incidents of purposeful, known, and ignored ethical violations. This type of conduct is too often permitted due to those who choose to be involved, are intimidated into silence, or determine the potential costs of involvement aren't worth it. The challenge is that complicit behavior (direct or indirect) is driven by a fear of getting involved, retaliation, or being labeled a snitch, which can prevent mindful actions that could stop wrongdoings, prevent a recurrence, and sometimes save lives if reported (even anonymously).

One of the biggest issues with ethical compliance is the presence of opportunity. The implementation of policies and procedures is a good starting point, but neither of these administrative items will prevent ethical misdoings without having ongoing independent processes and procedural reviews. Another preventative action to minimize the chances of administrative cover-up is to rotate individuals who are responsible for significant processes, financial, operational, or audit controls. By periodically shifting individual and/or organizational responsibilities, there are reduced opportunities to manipulate controls due to certain individuals using their insider knowledge for deceptive purposes.

There are various reasons for ethical violations, such as greed, intimidation, personal challenges, retaliation, workplace bullying, power, or other factors. These plentiful motivators can't always be identified until after the fact; nevertheless, there must be proactive and reactive mechanisms to quickly resolve any challenges prior to the emergence of bigger and more pervasive issues.

Ethical and unethical behavior can have negative costs and

outcomes. While thinking about unethical behavior, individuals usually and easily understand the impacts, such as damaged reputations, broken friendships, lost jobs, public scrutiny, emotional damage, depression, and death. Conversely, individuals don't often consider or can't imagine the negative impacts of ethical behavior, which interestingly can have similar consequences.

Ethical decision making is ultimately a personal choice; although, environmental influences (e.g., friends/family, religious institutions, organizations, cultures) can impact someone's willingness, desires, and actions. However, a decision to engage in unethical behavior is still an individual activity. Everyone should remember that... ethical behavior is pretty clear; the part that's gray is individual interpretation. Moreover, it's almost always better to review an earlier situation longing for a better outcome than to reflect on past actions with regret. The reason(s) someone chooses to be unethical covers a large spectrum, but many times it's tied to greed, self-esteem issues, and a desire to live beyond someone's means without honestly earning it. Notwithstanding, ethical behavior is a choice, an individual responsibility, and a reflection of the way someone wants to live their life.

My high school friend's reasons for choosing to be unethical might not ever be known. However, based on their various communications and Facebook messages prior to their death, there appeared to be a strong desire to project an image of status and extreme success. The unfortunate thing that many individuals (like my friend) realize too late is that material possessions are only a reflection of someone's financial status but cannot and will not reflect anyone's intrinsic worth. For my choices to be ethical and behave ethically, I lost a lot personally, professionally, and financially, including almost losing my life. Even though my experiences (as a result) were an arduous journey, I still have a strong belief and desire to do the right things regardless of any potential consequences. Although, I occasionally make bad choices. Despite all the devastatingly painful moments I experienced, I'm a better, more focused, socially conscientious, and driven man because of it.

Challenging moments and tough decisions are part of the human experience but choosing to be unethical or being complicit to unethical behavior isn't a winning solution. Short-term gains can be achieved by and through unethical acts, but… are the long-term consequences (direct/indirect) for yourself and others worth it? In the case of my high school friend, it appears that their unethical choices and behaviors led to the loss of a life. As for me, the tough decisions I made led to reclaiming mine, along with validating to myself and others that I am the man I say I am. The value, freedom, and confidence of this last consideration is absolutely and ethically priceless!

Defending Robin Williams' Death and Leveraging Facebook Helped Me to Rediscover My Light

The world was shocked to learn about Robin Williams' death and the manner in which he died two years ago. Mr. Williams death-by-suicide led to bewilderment on many different levels. The question many asked about his death was How could someone seemingly so happy and who brought happiness to many others die this way?

Too many individuals suffer silently and alone with some form of depression. A reason for this might be that there isn't enough information shared about the potential signs and effects of this disease. For me (at the time I started to feel depressed), I was familiar with the word depression but didn't understand its meaning, warning signs, or the devastating impact it can have on someone's life. The harsh reality is that untreated depression (in its worst forms) can result in death. According to the Centers for Disease Control and Prevention's 2014 National Center for Health Statistics, over the past 15 years, age-adjusted suicide rates increased by 24%.[17]

Around the world, countless individuals die every day due to fear, shame, and being told to suppress or not disclose their mental health challenges. These types of stigmas lead to this illness not being treated, unnecessary suffering, extended pain, and preventable deaths. No one should die because others make someone feel ashamed or unworthy because of a bona fide medical condition!

---

[17] Centers for Disease Control and Prevention's 2014 National Center for Health Statistics website at: cdc.gov/nchs/products/databriefs/db241.htm

Individuals who are affected by depression are sometimes told that they need to toughen up, they're being weak, called effeminate names, or other forms of degradation. It's interesting that these types of descriptors are used because pain, disappointment, and sorry happens to everyone. The manner in which emotions are processed varies, but sometimes the impacts of tough moments can cause prolonged feelings of extreme sadness.

Something that was said to me numerous times as I disclosed my mental health challenges was You were depressed; you always look so happy! I understood this sentiment, but there's a false perception that someone who is depressed will look, behave, or react a certain way. Nevertheless, if someone changes their normal routine (e.g., withdraws from regular activities, stops connecting with family/friends, becomes more isolated), then there might be a need to provide support[18]. However, don't push for disclosures, judge them, or compare their feelings to the way someone else might respond (including yourself).

Numerous individuals use fear as an excuse for inaction for themselves and others. It's understood that fear can be a barrier, but oftentimes it can be overcome by pushing (sometimes just a little) to take steps to make progress. Moreover, change can be uncomfortable, but silence can lead to unnecessary complacency that allows negative forces to prevail (internally or externally).

During my recovery, I used an unlikely tool… Facebook. This social media application that's sometimes condemned for

---

[18] Reference the article "Helping Someone Who Might Be Depressed".

allowing heartless attacks on it... changed and saved my life. I used Facebook (and my blog on The Huffington Post) as my personal diary for my emotional outlets and an extended support group; my first post "Depression – An Unnecessary Stigma[19]" was the hardest. Nevertheless, by sharing this article publicly, I visibly demonstrated to others (who might also be affected by depression) that they're not alone.

In the middle of the worst parts of my personal storms, I had mental turmoil, emotional damage, and financial/material losses. However, these impacts pale in comparison to the significant societal value I've added for myself and others by boldly, openly, and without reservations sharing the toughest moments of my life… my path to recover after a near-suicide.

Silence about my struggles led to personal and financial losses; however, a greater loss would have been for me to surrender and give-up by ending my life. In March 2014, I was minutes from doing so. In those moments which felt like an eternity, I called one of my brothers not to save myself but instead to ensure that our mother would be cared for after I was gone. This is yet another example that by caring for something or someone greater than myself… my life was saved. Without these feelings of caring and compassion, my life would have certainly ended that day.

During the hardest parts of my recovery, I reclaimed my life moment-by-moment by using writing to share my pain --- while also attempting to change viewpoints about mental health challenges. In the years since my depression began, I've addressed, brought awareness to, and challenged

---

[19] Reference the article "Depression – An Unnecessary Stigma".

stigmatic beliefs about depression/mental health, ethics, workplace bullying, criminal justice reform, and learning to live a fulfilled life.

I didn't want this treacherous, life-altering, and heart-wrenching experience by any means, but it's my mine; I own it! I could have surrendered to the pain, agony, and feelings of worthlessness by drinking, doing drugs, or any other reckless activities.; instead, I searched inward, purposely worked harder, and reclaimed my life. Being in the darkness of depression is a very lonely place, but each person must find their way back towards the light whether it's with counseling, drug therapy, prayer, writing, volunteering, or other positive outlets.

Whenever you're feeling bad, wanting to give-up, or thinking about ending your life, consider my quote entitled Darkness Fuels the Light:

> *Your darkest days don't define you, but instead provide an opportunity for you to display your strength and character, which will ultimately drive the individual you become.*

Today, I have clarity, purpose, passion, and direction. Prior to my depression and near-suicide, I went through the motions and lived someone else's life[20]. It hasn't been easy. At times, it's been an ongoing battle to get-up, keep moving, and remain positive. Conversely, if I stayed down or ended my life, I would have missed some incredible experiences[21]

---

[20] Reference the article "What If?!".

[21] Reference the article "Letter to Myself Written a Year Later".

these past couple of years, which began with learning who I am[22] and helping others to do the same.

I never imagined that a little over two years since my near-suicide, I would have authored a few books, would reach countless individuals by blogging on The Huffington Post, connected with various thought-leaders on my radio show Beyond Just Talk with S. L. Young, taught hundreds of inmates, and realized that regardless of my struggles my life still has value. Notwithstanding, the most important things I've done were to connect with individuals who are also dealing with depression, and those who lost loved ones that told me that my articles/books helped them to better understand mental health challenges.

Initially, I didn't have the strength to fight for myself after being beaten down by unethical workplace bullies for far too long. Although, it's interesting that my strength derived from reading a judgmental comment on Facebook about Robin Williams who was unnecessarily scrutinized (after his death) because of the manner in which he died. It was at this point, I said, "Enough!!!" I didn't get mad, but I unbelievably decided to share my journey to recover to help, change, inspire, and save lives.

Robin Williams… I didn't have the gift of meeting you, but in some distant ways I know you. I watched you as a child, laughed with/at you as an adult, and now understand that our untreated depression can kill. The true measure of a life isn't in the things that someone acquires, but instead by the value of the contributions left behind after their time is done.

---

[22] Reference the article "It's Still a Wonderful Life".

From the day we're born until the day we die, none of us lives alone or navigates life alone; therefore, we must be willing to support each other during sometimes very challenging times. Please know that your untimely death helped me to identify my light (for myself and others). For me Mr. Williams, I wouldn't be the man I am today without the light your life directed onto mine at a critical time that I was ready to put out my flame.

Don't be silent about your struggles, as silence can be deadly. If you're affected by depression, please get help and know that you're not alone. Also, remember that there's always someone, somewhere who is ready and willing to help.

Anyone who needs assistance should contact the Suicide & Crisis Lifeline at 988lifeline.org or 988.

Parting Thoughts

The same day and within hours of my near-suicide, I forced myself to leave my house to teach at a jail as scheduled --- at the urging of a friend. Even though the jail was closed to visitors that day, going to the jail was one of the best and most important things I've ever done. By choosing to continue to move forward despite my tenuous state-of-mind, I removed the focus from myself and redirected it toward someone else. Then, for a few moments, I thought about life beyond my situation at that time.

Life won't always be easy! There will be times that you'll want to yell, cry, or to identify other ways (e.g., mediation, helping others, pray) to release stress (hopefully in positive ways). Then, once the stress is reduced or released, quickly get back to living your life.

During the moments that you feel alone, don't have anyone to share your pain, or believe that the world is about to collapse upon you, please know that there's always someone who is ready, willing, and able to spend time, listen, and help you get through your challenging moment(s). The issue (many times) is being willing to allow someone an opportunity to help.

Surprisingly, I've done and accomplished more during the year following my near-suicide than I could have ever imagined to be possible. My accomplishments were achieved because I fought for my life, actively pursued my dreams, and refused to allow anyone's projections about me or my values to prevent me from achieving my positive dreams… without reservations.

I won't tell you that your year after a challenging period will be a better year, too; although, I will share that the quicker you make an active choice and subsequent decision to move forward… the sooner you'll have an opportunity to transform the thing(s) that hold you back into building blocks for progress. Then, these past challenges (over time) will become distant memories, as you work to build and have a better tomorrow.

Being vulnerable enough to share your pains shouldn't be an issue, challenge, or concern if you're surrounded by individuals who will love, protect, and be there to support you during your worst days (as well as your best)!

My extreme hope is that by sharing my journey with taboo topics such as depression and mental health, I will help to remove stigmas associated with these (and perhaps other) bona fide medical concerns.

As for me, my year-long writing project about my mental health challenges was done for self-healing and to help others during my journey toward living a happy, rewarding, fulfilled, meaningful, and purposeful life!

Best wishes for your future; I wish you nothing but the utmost success, a life consumed by the pursuit of your desires, and a lifetime of positive pursuits to achieve your dreams!

Please remember…

> *Don't allow anyone to cause you to question your worth --- no matter the negative action(s) someone might try to do to you.*

Finally, don't ever forget to always … be *your* best!

Epilogue

The following updates reflect on the extraordinarily surprising benefits of human connections whenever strangers (who share a common bond… which most of us do) allow their hearts, minds, and spirits to connect.

I never imagined that I would share my life (especially the worst parts of it) so openly. Yet, I somehow understood the importance of my work. I also considered that… if depression had such a devasting affect and effect on me, then could others learn from my journey?

Well, my answer was an overwhelming yes.

Therefore, over the past six years, I've documented the many lows and the amazing highs of actively choosing to fight for my life. It's interesting that the hardest parts of my challenges weren't related to living my life. Instead, it was in sharing the parts that would have helped me to live and have a better life.

Societal stigmas (real or perceived) need to be ended. This will ensure that everyone has a chance to feel and experience a full range of emotions that provide a greater spectrum throughout life. Nevertheless, it won't always be easy, but if we fight through the difficult moments… it can lead to a greater appreciation for the happier ones.

Along my journey, one of the life-altering and positive outcomes of my public mental health battle was related to meeting an incredible woman (Mrs. Mary Hanson). Over a five-year period, Mrs. Hanson and I shared our thoughts[23], pains, and desires to learn from the aftermath of suicidal ideation and death-by-suicide.

These new chapters reflect the growth that can occur while actively processing pain to purposely gain enlightenment.

Prior to my first communication with Mrs. Hanson, I had almost lost my hopes for humanity and the kindness of the human spirit. To be frank, I hated the world and everyone in it. Nevertheless, my collective emotional, mental, and spiritual journey with Mrs. Hanson proved that love is a powerful tool for recovery. Moreover, by having strong faith that things will improve, this belief can help to move us past difficult moments to learn, grow, be better, and hopefully become wiser.

My life and spirit are forever positively changed. During this journey, I risked myself to openly, boldly share painful commentaries about my experiences with severe depression and mental health challenges. Moreover, Mrs. Hanson validated that I and my story mattered. This steadfast support helped push me toward greater heights than I ever believed was possible… at least for me.

Love can be fleeting, but it can also be found in the most unexpected places if we allow our hearts, minds, and souls to be open to embrace the gifts of our commonalities and not our differences.

---

[23] Listen to my 2016 interview with Mrs. Hanson on my radio show: mixcloud.com/beyondjusttalk/beyond-just-talk-with-s-l-young_110616

We must always remember that… love is love is love!

Sharing Pain Leads to Building New Family Connections

As I reflect today (June 2020) on the six years since my near-suicide, my feelings are of gratitude and thankfulness for being able to survive. It wasn't easy to navigate the many highs and lows related to overcoming my severe depression. However, I'm fortunate to have learned invaluable lessons that rebuilt me and were shared with others to help them to do the same.

Vulnerability Opens Hearts

During these turbulent years, there was one surprising person who supported me emotionally and with a mother's love. This remarkable woman is Mary Hanson.

Mrs. Hanson contacted me after reading my article "Letter to Myself the Day Before My Near-Suicide: Written a Year Later," which was published on The Huffington Post (now the HuffPost) in March 2014. This piece memorialized my journey from a broken man to one who was determined to move forward (during a period of considerable pain) and help others, too.

Mrs. Hanson's email (days after my article appeared) echoed through my soul. It was an unimaginable response to my heart-wrenching reflection on a year's arduous journey that wasn't considered by me (and perhaps many others) to be possible.

In her email, she wrote:

I don't know if my e-mail will find you. I don't belong to Facebook, Twitter, etc.

Your Huffington Post blog was absolutely beautiful and touched my soul deeply. Thank goodness you listened to that little voice to reach out bit by bit. It was so valuable to me, you sharing the timeline and what beautiful things came to you after the crisis.

I have struggled most of my life. My children were my saviors, motivating my inner voice to seek treatment and a healthier path... a work in progress.

My beautiful 26 year old son chose to end his life three years ago, a week before his birthday. We held a funeral instead of a birthday party on his special day. I had talked with him on the phone that evening and he would not give up any info other than he wasn't feeling right. He could not describe to me what was going on physically/mentally. Before we hung up I said I love you.

Local police stopped by at 5 am to say my son had committed suicide. This was a shock for the most part...but not...he was a giver, hard worker... survivor... his career had recently taken off... he had a ton of friends, participated in sports and kept fit... BUT also realized communication and his understanding of people skills was a challenge for him.... along with many events from his past...a perfect storm culminated if you will.

This is why I could never be angry with his decision, gapingly sad-yes. However miracles do happen and our family has recognized them each and every day. We did the family work via therapy, worked hard and came out on the

> *other side intact and experiencing goodness no one ever could imagine. The power of loving and forgiving yourself, and others, keeping ego and its negativity at bay are lessons I wish I would have known forty years ago.*
>
> *Thanks again......sending love your way...*

This email validated my gut-wrenching decision to be bold enough to share my journey to reclaim my life after being moments from ending it. This amazing God-sent confirmation taught me that the worst parts of my life and story could (and did) help others.

A Mother's Pain

In an email years later, Mrs. Hanson provided additional insights about her son (Brian) who died-by-suicide on February 12, 2012.

> *It started with a phone call to my son. After several tries over the course of a week, Brian finally answered the phone at 7 p.m. He said, Mom, I'm not feeling well. I asked, what was wrong; why aren't you feeling well? He replied, I don't know.*
>
> *Our conversation was brief... no more than 5 to 10 minutes. I ended our call by saying I love you.*
>
> *After the call, I felt sad and wondered if my son still loved me. During our brief talk, he was so reserved. Afterward, I debated whether I should call back, but decided not to do it to give him space to deal with whatever was happening.*

That night, I went to bed with a heavy heart. At midnight, Brian sent a final text message to his sister, which simply said: I love you - you've been a really good sister. Tell Mom I love her. A short time later, he sent another text to his roommate with the message You've been a good friend.

At 5 a.m., my husband and I were woke-up by our doorbell buzzing. At the door, there were two police officers with the unbearable news that that our son had ended his life at approximately 2 a.m. The officers then provided the contact name and number for the detective assigned to the case (in the city that our son lived).

Our hearts and souls felt like they were violently ripped from our bodies. The room went dark for me. Suddenly, there was a shift in my thinking that everything I believed to be true and needed in my life were no longer so. Game over; we didn't imagine that our son's suicide would be our reality.

At 6 a.m., we started to make phone calls to let the family know about Brian's death. The first call was to our daughter. She couldn't believe that her brother was gone. Frantically, she checked her phone and sadly found Brian's text that was sent at midnight. Devastated by this reality, she gathered her belongings and came to our home.

As the day went on, additional calls were made to our closest family and friends. Each responded literally by screaming No; this can't be true! While making these calls, I could only bare to tell them that Brian died-by-suicide, as it wasn't possible to provide any further details at that time.

The only comfort – during this nightmare – was having our family and friends scrambled to our home to support our family during these life-changing moments in which our world stopped.

Mrs. Hanson also wrote the following message for her son (Brian) to be included with this update.

To Brian...

We brought you lovingly into this world almost 27 years to the day of your death.

We wanted to ensure that you were taken care of properly and lovingly sent back to the creator.

We prayed for you and your peace.

We took care of your estate and legal matters.

We cleaned your apartment and had the space blessed.

Your service was absolutely beautiful! It was filled with love from a large community that was devastated by your absence.

Your service was on your birthday.

We were never angry or ashamed.

It didn't matter why you chose this path, really; sometimes things are just as it is without explanation or justification.

The need to know melted away, as it wouldn't change the outcome or bring you back.

We experience signs that you are still with us, which is comforting.

Because of your choice, our family made a conscious decision to do the work to heal and move forward in a positive direction; both together and separately. You were the sole catalyst for the change that needed to happen.

We miss you desperately... but we're thankful for the gifts and miracles that were left in the wake, and that continue to come to us.

I will always love you my son.

Mom

Support Goes Both Ways

In one of my emails to Mrs. Hanson on February 12, 2019 (on the seventh year of her son's death), I wrote:

I hope you're doing okay!

Over the last few days, you were constantly on my mind as today's date approached. I know that this might be a challenging day. Notwithstanding, I'm sure that Brian wouldn't want you to focus on his passing, but instead to focus on the happiness surrounding his life and the blessing of his heart that he brought to yours.

This period is reflective for me too, as approximately a month from today I almost ended my life. Around the first year after my near-suicide, I wrote my article Letter to Myself the Day Before My Near-Suicide: Written a Year Later. This was one of the hardest things I've done or written, as I reflected on my journey into/out of darkness due to depression --- while dealing with the stigmas associated with discussing mental health. Nevertheless, I'm grateful that I pushed myself to write this piece --- for myself and the countless individuals like yourself who benefited from my painful disclosures.

In March 2015, you wrote me an email after reading this article. I never imagined in writing it or in responding to you that these experiences would change my life. It's interesting that (as I learned through our many conversations) that you didn't know a way to communicate with Brian during his suffering a few hours before his untimely death. Yet, you communicated clearly with me to let me know that I mattered, my contributions mattered, and that I was a positive force that could help many others. You blanketed me (this stranger) with a mother's love, compassion, and thoughtfulness. While addressing your pain, you extended your arms over distant miles to hug, hold, positively change, and love me.

Unfortunately, you couldn't save Brain... but, you saved me and my life. For this I will forever be grateful!

Also, it's interesting that you know the way that I look, I know the way Brian looked, but (by choice) I don't know the way you look. As we discussed years ago, I don't want to know the way you look until we meet in-person. With that said, next month will be the fifth year since I almost ended my life... and I want us to meet. This will give me an opportunity to hug my other mom (you) to tell her... I'm thankful for the years of love, support, and understanding... and that I love her, too.

Thank you for supporting me as I fought to hold on to and reclaim this valuable gift of life!"

One of the most incredible things about our shared journey was my inability (by choice) to see Mrs. Hanson's face, even though I already knew and felt her loving spirit.

The Meeting

After five years of phone calls and correspondence, I was finally ready to meet Mrs. Hanson. However, due to the coronavirus pandemic, our in-person meeting was delayed to protect us from possible infection. Nevertheless, we were still committed to meeting virtually for the first time, which occurred on 6/24/20. This meeting renewed my spirit and allowed our souls to further connect in ways I couldn't imagine to be possible.

Reflecting on the Shared Healing

In the days following our meeting, I couldn't stop thinking about the incredible journey that we collectively had to help each other heal. I also reflected on my decision to not want to know the way Mrs. Hanson looked until we met. After our virtual connection, my reasons for our unusual relationship were solidified.

For both of us, we had each other to help process some of the devastating effects of depression and the impact of suicide/suicidal ideation. This allowed us to better understand and address the underlying issues associated with our own mental health challenges.

For Mrs. Hanson, she had an opportunity to process her pain and the emotions of losing a son while also helping this man to recover in a way that only a mother can do.

For me, I had someone special who focused on our common bond.

This beautiful and highly unexpected relationship strengthened my desire to be better despite being moments from almost ending my life not that many years ago.

By not seeing Mrs. Hanson's face, it freed me to focus solely on the messaging, love, and support. In the void of not having a physical being to see, I was alone with her words that navigated through my soul. This artificial distance allowed me to be consumed (in the dark) with this affirming voice that gently caressed my emotions and soul with motherly compassion.

During a critical period in my recovery, it was if I was a protected embryo in an amniotic sac. The voice was familiar and warm, but I didn't really know to whom it belonged. This was my safe place to just be surrounded by love. Then, upon emerging from this protected haven, I was finally able to see[24] the mother who nurtured me back to life.

It's an experience that I will never forget, as it was the moment that the radiating energy from our souls fully connected.

---

[24] Watch the long-awaited meeting between S. L. Young and Mary Hanson after 5-years of supporting each other at: youtu.be/julQfbTxX4k

*****

To Mrs. Hanson:

Sadly, you lost your son; yet, you selfishly and continuously helped to love me back to life.

For your unrelenting love for others and for this man (along with so many more intangibles), I thank you with everything I am. If it wasn't for your unwavering support, then I might not be alive today. Also, I wouldn't have had an opportunity to positively impact countless lives.

From my entire soul and with blessings from beyond, I'm incredibly blessed to have another friend, supporter, and mother.

THANK YOU MOM!!!

Love your other son!

Reflections on My Battle to Save and Reclaim My Life

For so many years, I needlessly suffered alone. I falsely believed that it was better to deal with my challenges on my own. Isn't this the thing that strong people do?! Well, I was wrong... very much so!

Strength isn't defined by someone's ability to handle issues on their own, as strong people allow others to help them without worrying about a perception of weakness or being judged. This is an invaluable lesson I wished I put into practice a long time ago.

During my worst moments, unbelievably, the hardest part wasn't taking actions to get better; instead, it was telling family and friends that I was depressed and struggling. It's interesting that I wanted to get better, but my ego caused me to worry more about appearances, perceptions, and being judged than allowing those who really care about me to assist.

There's something inherently wrong with anyone having to second-guess disclosing any mental health challenges due to stigmatic beliefs. It's outdated thinking that makes individuals believe that it's worse (often by multitudes) to admit to a mental versus a physical ailment. This type of thinking is absurd! Anyone who has anything wrong with their body (emotional, physical, or mental) should immediately pursue treatment for any bona fide health condition. Furthermore, others' negative thoughts and/or commentaries shouldn't be an inhibitor or a barrier for anyone to seek or receive assistance.

For me, once I posted information about my battle with depression and near-suicide on Facebook[25] in August 2014, this was the moment that my life began to change.

For way too long, I didn't want anyone to know that I was struggling mentally, emotionally, financially, spiritually, and sometimes physically. However, once I disclosed and released the challenges that essentially held me as a prisoner within my own body, I immediately felt better and lighter. No longer was I burdened with trying to keep my secrets hidden. Furthermore, the most beneficial thing experienced was that family, friends, and amazingly strangers supported me and my journey to get better.

My recovery process is extremely extraordinary. It's shocking that the things that I was afraid to do (reveal my mental health and financial challenges) were the disclosures that helped me the most.

A week or so after posting my message on Facebook, one of my very close friends (Maggie Linton, former host of "The Maggie Linton Show" on SiriusXM) accepted my offer to discuss my battle with depression on her show[26].

Being interviewed on a nationally syndicated radio program was emotionally overwhelming and physically draining. Yet, this heart-wrenching outlet was an enormous relief. I felt a tremendous feeling of joy a short while after the show ended. Afterward, I communicated with countless individuals who

---

[25] Reference the article "Depression – An Unnecessary Stigma".

[26] Listen to this interview at: youtu.be/dUi2IQxcHrM

were impacted by my story or shared with me information about their struggles with mental health. These strong connections changed my perceptions about myself, my strength, my outreach, and the benefits that could be achieved by my encouraging others to discuss their challenges.

These were the moments that solidified my desire to help others and began my quest to raise awareness to the importance of mental health (along with addressing other stigmatic issues such as ethics and workplace bullying).

Now (looking back in 2020), I am incredibly blessed, thankful, and grateful that I didn't end my life. It's shocking to me today that I almost died-by-suicide because I believed that I was worthless and didn't have anything to offer that any might want from me.

For many years, I mistakenly believed that I was a failure, and that life couldn't/wouldn't get any better. I was in a tremendously dark place. Still, 2 – 3 hours after giving-up hope and wanting to die, I found refuge at a place that many don't want to go and often shun the people who reside there. This place is a jail[27].

Even though I felt worthless inside my heart, body, and soul. I made a purposeful choice to live… one moment at a time… as my brother (Johnnie) directed me to do.

After being comforted and swayed by a very close friend, I hesitantly mustered the strength to go to a local jail to teach inmates. By just leaving my house, I created a very much

---

[27] Read the article "Beyond the Clothes" at: slyoung.com/beyond-clothes

needed success and began to demonstrate my value. This was a powerful lesson that while my belief in myself was shattered, there was still an opportunity to help others (if I allowed myself to do it). It was in these feelings that my heart and emotions shifted to believe that I just might have something of value to offer others.

Even so, I knew that if I decided to die by suicide then I wouldn't know if my positive actions could or would make a difference for myself and others. Therefore, I reluctantly put my heart and soul into giving-back to opportunity (at-risk) communities, which ultimately taught me that losing the things I lost didn't really matter. The most significant thing in that moment was that I still had life and an ability (if I chose) to uplift myself and others who needed hope, too.

I'd like to take credit for my decision to start teaching inmates in October 2013, but this wouldn't be true. I did, however, make a choice to follow the direction of family and friends to use my books from the "It's a Crazy World… Learn From It" series[28] with inmates. Although, it's laughable now, my response to their direction was "You want me to take inspirational quotes… to a jail… to teach inmates; yeah, right!" Fortunately, I listened to their advice because it was at the Arlington County Detention Facility in Arlington, VA that I learned that positive things can and do happen just by showing-up.

Jails are generally considered to be places for bad people who deserve to be punished for their actions and crimes. Alas, this

---

[28] These books were written (as I started to enter a period of deep depression) as a tool to help myself to learn from my experiences and remain positive.

is the type of thinking that sometimes prevents many inmates from receiving help, pivotal services, and opportunities for redemption upon their release.

How does society expect improved behavior and futures for these people upon release unless socialization, education, and mental health services are provided during their sentence?![29]

Numerous incarcerated people didn't have access to a quality education and/or positive role models to provide guidance. Therefore, this work (for me) is about repaying a debt due to the countless family members, educators, counselors, and friends who helped a misguided young man refocus his juvenile energy toward education versus perfecting my criminal activities. These life-saving and transformational interventions cannot ever be fully repaid.

During my first visit to the jail to determine if I would be able and wanted to teach inmates, I had a serendipitous encounter. After taking a few steps into the housing unit, someone called my real name (as I go by a nickname these days). I didn't recognize the voice, so I kept walking. Then, the person called my name again. This time, I slowly turned with a look of bewilderment to determine who was calling me. Shockingly, it was an old friend who I hung-out with during high school. This chance encounter was a definitive sign that this place (that I was apprehensive about entering) was the location that I was supposed to be to make a meaningful difference.[30]

---

[29] Reference Appendix G: Inmate Management: What's Wanted Better Criminals or Citizens?

[30] Read the article "Lessons Learned From 9 Months Voluntarily Locked-Up" at: slyoung.com/voluntarily-lockedup

My first jail visit was in February 2013 with my inaugural class started in October 2013. Then, approximately five months later, it was going to this facility on that fateful day that saved my life (at least at that time) because people were expecting me. It was this feeling of being needed, which was just enough to begin my initial steps toward recovery.

Almost seven years later, some of my greatest life's joys came from teaching, helping, and inspiring over 500 inmates to consider their current circumstances as challenges to be overcome and not permanent destinations.

One of the most important lessons that I teach these students is that others will attempt to put limitations on you, your abilities, and your future, but don't accept this as your belief or compound these views by adding your own. Additionally, I shared with them lived-experiences based on my proven abilities to overcome severe educational and mental health challenges to excel.

The significant takeaway from my onerous journeys is that things won't always be easy, but your attitude and perspective about the things being done or pursued will be much better if you proceed as if it's impossible to fail. Just by removing this mental limitation and moving forward anyway, you'll already be further along and more importantly have achieved some success.

I'm still absolutely amazed that by being vulnerable (about my challenges and spending time with those incarcerated) that these experiences had a monumental positive impact on me and transformed my life.

My choices to be extremely transparent about the worst parts of my life are considered (by some) to be too personal to share and for others to be societal taboos to discuss so openly. For me, by sharing my feelings and spending time in a jail, these faithful choices provided the necessary shock to my system that caused a reboot that was critical to drive further, positive, and life-altering changes.

It's sometimes believed that individuals must be at their bottom before they're ready to rebound. I don't necessarily agree with these claims. Nevertheless, the significant message is that by stripping away the layers and complexities related to worrying about being judged, it allows us to be and embrace who we truly are as humans. This understanding helps to further our compassion related to accepting that everyone has challenges to overcome.

Therefore, let's not create unnecessary barriers for anyone to allow themselves to be fully seen and/or unnecessarily condemned for things that any of us could experience or be in the same negative position. It's in our appreciation for humanity and providing opportunities for redemption that we can/will evolve as a society to collectively expand our shared strengths.

A Second Chance at Life Led to Learning Ways to Purposefully Live

Never, ever, could I have imagined that this one-time broke and broken man who believed his life was worthless (that no one wanted anything that he had and wanted to end his life in March 2014) would amazingly transform this near tragedy from a nightmare into an inspirational story of hope. These positive changes were driven by my faith, desires, determination, resolve, perseverance, and resilience to move forward to rebuild my life into one focused on giving-back to others.

It's extremely unfortunate that it took almost dying before I discovered my worth and purpose for living. Too many times, our future and dreams are aligned with limited perspectives about ways to achieve our desires. Additionally, the answers to our questions about life and associated curiosities aren't always received in the way in which these might be wanted or expected. Therefore, our perspectives must be broadened to identify opportunities and an openness to receive enlightenment in various ways, including places and times that might not be imagined.

My Mental Health Decline

Over the years, I seldom discussed the specific reasons that led me to almost end my life. Yet, in this new chapter, I know it's time to finally share this part of my story. This revelation provides insights and considerations about the sudden onset of severe depression and the risks of not seeking proper, timely medical attention.

I'll start by sharing that my desire to end my life wasn't planned. Yes, I had suicidal ideation. Yes, I wanted the considerable, ongoing pain to end. Nevertheless, I wanted (and still do want) to live. However, I just couldn't identify a way to get past my career and financial challenges related to my desire to be ethical, along with my inability to secure professional opportunities and income to support myself, respectively.

The issues that plagued me were intensified because of the blatant incongruence between the company or organizational environments in which I worked and the proclaimed societal expectations.

The direction received from my family, schools, organizations, societies, religion, and my heart's inclinations were to always "do the right thing(s)." However, whenever I conformed with supposed expectations for societal norms, then troubles repeatedly consumed my orbit. These self-imposed challenges were directly related to my unyielding desire to be ethical, stand-up for myself, speak-out against wrongdoings, and be a good person. Nevertheless, these significant juxtapositions of differing, questionable expected outcomes inhibited my abilities to determine viable options to improve my situation.

The Breaking Point

At my lowest point in March 2014, I didn't have gainful employment, my limited salary didn't cover my expenses, and my retirement account was depleted. My breaking point happened once I was sued by a creditor for my delinquency and inability to make my credit card payments.

Prior to addressing unethical activities at serval companies (as required by my employers and credentials), for over a decade, I earned a mid-to-high six figure salary. Then, once the summons to appear in court arrived, I believed that I was a failure, no one wanted anything that I was, could do, or could be. Furthermore, I convinced myself that my personal value would be exponentially increased by being dead rather than alive.

This onslaught of mental and emotional assaults on my soul, worth, and identity broke me. I was a deflated, distraught, and defeated man whose mind broke. Now, my emotions were overwhelmed, and my fight to live was gone. Then, the sudden pressing message generated from deep within my soul was that I needed to die (now).

Fortunately, one of my brothers recognized my medical emergency and reacted in time to save my life. Then, my sister helped to regain my focus on the things that needed to be done to get past the current crisis. Both actions were extremely important. Yet, perhaps the most critical advice received was from a very good friend who pushed me to go to a jail to teach my class as planned. This decision to move forward roughly 3 – 5 hours after nearly ending my life was the hardest thing I have ever done. In an inconceivably short time after being moments from ending my life, I (with the help of family and a friend) mustered the courage to do something implausible and positive by deciding to maintain my commitment to teach inmates that afternoon. Nevertheless, the powerful lesson in this action was that even if I couldn't help myself... I still could help someone else.

Rediscovering My Value

Even with this manufactured strength, I didn't teach my students that afternoon because the jail was on lockdown. Notwithstanding, by simply going to the jail, I began the initial steps to reclaim my life and demonstrate my life's value. Oftentimes, change begins by taking just one step followed by another to start momentum to begin a period of transformation. Even so, it won't always be easy, but by simply getting started... you've created a new success.

During the challenging years, my immediate focus centered around my material losses, which were incorrectly given greater importance than my mental well-being. Therefore, the more the financial losses compounded, the greater my internal perception of worthlessness, and the self-perceived increasingly outward appearance of me being a failure escalated.

The reality was that I wasn't a failure or a worthless man! Instead, I was temporarily broken, needed assistance, and was desperately in need of repair. Yet, something I absolutely needed to remember the most was that I still had value, an ability to improve myself, and ample opportunities to better my future. Furthermore, during these challenging times, I never lost myself or who I want to be. Even while it would have been easy to change the person that I was to conform and maintain excellent compensation (in multiple companies). I, rightfully, chose to remain true to my beliefs, faith, and myself regardless of the potential negative outcomes.

By not losing myself while many unethical people existed in

my orbit, I realized that personal worth doesn't come from the values possessed, but by… who you are; what you believe; what you do? By knowing during the tough moments of my life who I really am, it led to me not losing the most important asset I have… me.

> <u>Note:</u> One of the many powerful lessons that my mother taught me was… Folks can take almost everything from you, but *never lose your dignity or self-respect to anyone… ever.* Little did I know that this message would become an important battle cry to justify and sustain my ability to maintain my desired ethical positions without compromising my beliefs or values.

The Initial Steps Toward Recovery

During the many years of my severe depression, I reflected on and reevaluated who I was as a person, man, and contributor. Once these roles were clearly understood, it caused me to actively pursue my dreams instead of being stifled by the burden of lost jobs, cash, assets, and friends.

The darkest moments in my life were used to understand and better define who I am as a person and man. I relentlessly sought to live on purpose by doggedly working on developing my dreams and passions, which transformed the way I saw myself, the world, and my place in it. During this period of upheaval, I committed to building a better me.[31]

---

[31] Listen to Dr. Young's 2020 interview on the "Oh My Goff Show" with Angie Goff: youtu.be/aFNWvUR1dg8

Moment-by-moment, step-by-step, and day-by-day, I learned that my positive choices were critical to my recovery, actions needed to be willfully future focused, and maintaining a mindset necessary to be prepared for tough battles to conquer my internal demons. Therefore, my mantra that was repeated throughout this period was "Keep moving forward!"

Preparing for Growth

While working to rebuild myself and my confidence, writing was my release; it also served as my therapy. These reflections caused me to explore the negative effects of being conditioned to project certain outward appearances (e.g., toxic masculinity).

As men, we're taught to suppress emotions[32]. This outdated, senseless, and limited thinking has caused too many people (especially men) to suffer alone in silence. Notwithstanding, the amazing thing that I quickly learned by openly sharing my challenges was that a few of my friends/family were negatively impacted by debilitating depression, too.

These numerous private conversations strengthened my resolve to publicly share more about my mental health struggles and recovery to encourage others to do something to help themselves to heal.

My unbridled strength to be so open came from a quote by an unknown person that invigorated my position, which is "No one has ever died from embarrassment, and you won't be the

---

[32] Reference the article "Why Shouldn't Men Cry?!" in Appendix E.

first." This quote empowered me and gave myself permission to explore many options by taking calculated risks.

Interesting observations emerged during my recovery:

- The first lesson was that people are usually willing to help someone whenever they're in an extreme struggle. However, as I recovered, I noticed an interesting paradox that my supporters decreased with my sudden increasing successes. Then, as I surpassed others' expectations and/or wants for my recovery, I found that my supporters (including new ones) weren't as visible. Although, my true supporters were always there during the good, bad, ugly, challenging, and questionable times. For this ongoing assistance and encouragement, I'm extremely thankful to and for all of them.

- The second lesson, a critical one, is that by owning my story and telling it my way... no one owned me. Too many times, individuals are held back because someone knows a secret about them that's used to control, manipulate, intimidate, or abuse them. Based on this cumulative reflection, I decided that (after being moments from ending my life which was already extraordinarily costly and almost broke me emotionally, financially, spiritually) I would do and be me... for me. Therefore, I rebuilt myself on my terms and in my own way without worrying about others' commentaries (negative or otherwise) about me. This change stopped me from second-guessing myself and allowed me to live without unnecessary fears, doubts, or worries.

The amazing thing about my journey is that I absolutely learned who I really am. Prior to the challenging times, I ran around doing a lot of unnecessary and time-wasting things, but *I failed to get to know myself and who I wanted to be.* Once my ego was checked to allow myself to be vulnerable about my depression and the circumstances that led to it, I then gave myself permission to take calculated risks that led to unimaginable and unexpected growth.

My New Perspective

In the approximately four years that I felt worthless and believed that nobody wanted anything from me or my services, I learned to evolve setbacks into triumphs by choosing to mindfully live. I stopped worrying about the things that others said, did, or the negative voices that often negatively affected my progress.

My new, assertive strategy to move forward is to address issues as soon as possible versus not dealing with them. I also deflect useless commentary (even from myself), and act with positive beliefs that anything I want to achieve is possible (and even if it isn't achievable, then I've learned during the process). Furthermore, I shifted my mindset to effectively use my time, energy, and effort to commit to doing things fully with an understanding that everything I want won't happen as or at the time I desire it to occur. This life-altering realization reshaped one of my critical beliefs that...

There's always value in a positive journey, even if the outcome isn't as wanted or expected.

In the six years since I fought for my life, I (for example):

- Was a contributor on The Huffington Post;

- Delivered a commencement address in the school district in which I was directed to leave high school in the tenth grade after failing 6 of 7 classes and missing approximately 1/3 of the school year;

- Was a radio host for two programs;

- Wrote fourteen books;

- Was published in college textbooks;

- Became a university professor in addition to teaching at a community college;

- Taught over 2,000 students (including 500+ inmates);

- Developed a course (based on my life) for incoming freshman at a university to develop their foundational strengths;

- Was a keynote speaker and featured presenter at several corporate/professional events;

- Received three notable awards for teaching incarcerated students:
    - Volunteer of the Month award at a local jail;
    - Distinguished Service Award from the organization Leadership Arlington;
    - The Martin Luther King, Jr. Innovative Service Award from the U.S. Department of Education in conjunction with the White House Initiative for Educational Excellence for African Americans;
- Delivered a graduation address at a jail for students earning their General Equivalency Diploma (GED);
- Delivered a graduation address at a private high school;
- Inducted into two academic organizations: The Honor Society of Phi Kappa Phi and The Honor Society of Kappa Delta Pi;
- Earned my doctorate degree in Educational Leadership and Organizational Innovation with a 4.0 Grade Point Average (GPA).

If I needlessly ended my life in 2014, then none of these accomplishments could or would have been possible, along with not having an ability to positively impact countless lives around the world.

The Power of Hope and Positivity

If there's one main lesson from my story/journey, then it's that...

> *Hope is a powerful tool that can help move us forward, even during our darkest days. Just a little of it can embolden individuals to act and move toward achieving a goal, which can also lead to other successes that encourages further actions.*

Inactivity and aimlessly wandering don't normally lead to positive changes, but by purposely choosing to live... it begins a process that directs our time, energy, and effort toward the future, which happens to be the place that we'll spend the rest of our lives.

One of my new quotes and mantras that keeps me inspired and drives my motivation today is...

> *The biggest positive risks that anyone should take is on themselves. So many people never achieve their dreams due to fear, which can cause them to live a life of regret. Therefore, don't be one of them... go big, bold, and move boundlessly.*

My Message for You

I hope that my journey to fight for my life provides inspiration for you to make reflective changes in yours.

We must always remember that things won't always be good or easy. Although, positive things can and do happen, by addressing issues as soon as practicable and taking actions to move past them. Moreover, in moving forward with belief and faith, progress begins to transform a moment into momentum to positively change your life... and perhaps others, too.

Letter to Myself the Day Before My Near-Suicide Written Almost Seven Years Later

*****

With the completion of the previous update to this book, I believed that I had written and reflected on almost everything about my journey into darkness and recovery back into the light. Yet, with the many challenges and ensuing struggles brought on in 2020 due to the coronavirus or COVID-19 pandemic, I understood that an additional update was necessary. Therefore, this new section provides a positive perspective about the power of not losing yourself even though financial and/or material things are lost.

*****

During the height of your career as a program manager, you worked with individuals who were unethical, lacked morals, used their power to circumvent processes/procedures, engage in nepotism, bullied workers, and more. However, you were taught to do the right things(s), protect those who can't/don't protect themselves, and not become complicit to these actions by being silent. Following the guidance received from family/friends, churches, schools, colleges/universities, companies, organizations, and societies, you'll do as directed. Yet, you will painfully learn that being ethical and an upstanding person aren't easy, requires dogged commitment, and will have life-altering consequences.

You repeatedly had to determine whether you would go-along to get-along and adjust your moral compass to maintain a paycheck. However, this isn't something that you were willing to do. You correctly understood that adjusting your ethical framework (even slightly) would change who you are and who you want to be. These decisions weren't easy to make because these ethical dilemmas continuously emerged. Nevertheless, you consistently chose to leave well-paying jobs instead of becoming like those who aggressively attacked or didn't protect you for not agreeing to do the same. You were not willing to be complicit through silence.

As the significant weight of the consequences related to your ethical choices permeate your mind, body, and soul, you're drained, disgusted, defeated, depressed, and distraught. These ethical battles and the enormous stress caused you to withdraw from living life, drained your savings, led to severe depression, and kept you unemployed for years. As the pressure grows, you can't imagine withstanding the ongoing debilitating pain and continuous nightmares that seemingly will never end.

These feelings are a distant place from the plentiful life you lived a few years ago. At that time, you had a great job managing multi-million dollar projects, were making a good six-figure salary, and were living the life you worked relentlessly to build. Currently, you can't pay your bills, you're embarrassed, you're broke, and you believe that no one wants anything from you. Furthermore, next week, you're scheduled to have judgments entered against you in debtors court since you cannot afford to pay any of them.

Today, you'll begin to succumb to the feelings of despair without any hope that things will get better. In this moment, you finally comprehend and fully understand the expression "I'm worth more dead than alive," as your personal value is falsely and incorrectly tied to your financial standing and life insurance policy. This unfortunate situation will be your breaking point. Suddenly, your connection to reality and hopes that the future could or would be any better have quickly disappeared.

You can only reflect on the many ethical decisions you made that were supposedly aligned with the things that good people do. Nevertheless, every time you did these things you were attacked, questionably judged, scrutinized, isolated, condemned, ousted, and found yourself repeatedly alone on the outside looking inward.

After steadfastly committing to being ethical, doing the right things, and always experiencing negative backlashes to these unbelievable challenges, you're broke, depressed, emotionally scorned, mentally exhausted, physically debilitated, and wondering… "Why me?!" Then, the thoughts will digress into asking yourself… "Why should I continue to fight anymore?!" and "Why do I want to live in a world that attacks me for doing the things that I was taught and trained to ethically do?!"

Your answer to the last question is… "Life is no longer worth living if there isn't any good left in the world (at least for me) and things keep getting exponentially worse." At this moment, you will surrender to your perceived failures, inability to make a positive influence, inability to add any value, and increased desire to die.

Even though you're beaten, bruised, and battered, you will rebound if you have… a little belief that things can get better (it doesn't take much), faith that this isn't the way your life is supposed to end (this could be the beginning of something unexpected and beautiful), commitment to finding ways to do something positive (your experiences can help others), and determination to transform this near-tragedy into an amazing transformation (you can't participate in the future if you're not alive to experience it).

Now that you're starting to think differently... brace yourself, as tomorrow will be the worst moment of your life.

It will start with you not wanting to get out of bed. You won't be able to focus. You will experience a psychosis, which will make you begin to have suicidal ideations. You will convince yourself that you're a failure and you don't have any value or worth. You will prepare for your death.

As you begin to finalize your actions, you'll call one of your brothers to ensure that your mother will be cared for after you're dead. Although, you can't complete the call without getting upset and crying. Your brother will ask questions and you will hastily hang-up the phone. Your brother will call back again and again to try to reach you, but you won't answer. Then, in a moment of sanity, you return your brother's calls. During the conversation, he will remind you that... "... this is just a moment; you need to get past this moment."

You will be teetering between life and death, as you hear a rhythmical chant telling you repeatedly to "Do it, do it, do it, ..." Fortunately, your brother (who calls for over an hour until he reaches you) will help you begin to reconnect with reality and understand that life could get better if you fight to get through this moment.

Listen to me! I know that you don't want to die, and you're in a lot of pain. Please understand that it's not easy to do the right things and none of us are perfect. However, in fighting against wrongful acts, you've changed and grown in immeasurable ways that you don't understand or realize. Notwithstanding, if you push through this pain and moment, then things will get better. I know it's hard to believe, but trust me, I know it will happen. The work you will do based on your hard-learned life lessons is worthy, valuable, and will help countless individuals in ways that you can't even imagine.

You won't feel or believe this today, but years from now you will embrace the challenges that you experienced because it made you stronger and better. These experiences provide unique perspectives that you didn't have and will allow you to better connect with many individuals and organizations that you will soon provide meaningful services. This might seem unbelievable today, but trust me, you will leverage your painful lived-experiences to help, inspire, and uplift thousands of people (many who you will never meet) through publications, radio shows (including your own), television shows, speaking engagements, and much more.

In the first year after your near-suicide (Read article "Letter to Myself the Day Before My Near-Suicide Written a Year Later,"[33] you will speak with an audience about having belief in yourself, write a book to document the impact of unethical individuals on mental health, begin to publicly share (e.g., radio, printed media, television) your mental health

---

[33] Reference the article "Letter to Myself the Day Before My Near-Suicide Written A Year Later".

challenges, become a mentor to a high school student, be asked to be a commencement speaker in a school district in which you almost didn't graduate, be an alumni panelist at a school you took non-degree classes to prove that you belong, and many other things.

Now, let's look beyond the first year to see the absolutely amazing things that are in your future if you don't make a horrible choice to end your life tomorrow.

First, you will deliver a commencement address in the same district that directed you to leave high school in the tenth grade. Even better, your mentee will graduate at the same ceremony.

Second, you will start your radio show "Beyond Just Talk with S. L. Young" to discuss meaningful topics to educate, inform, uplift, inspire, and enlighten.

Third, articles you write on The Huffington Post will be published in higher education textbooks.

Fourth, after eight years of trying, you will become a university professor.

Fifth, you will independently develop a university course for incoming freshman to teach them methods and strategies to develop their own foundational strengths.

Sixth, you will receive three distinguished awards for your work teaching over 500 inmates. These are the "Volunteer of the Month" at a local jail, "Martin Luther King, Jr. Innovative Service Award" in conjunction with the White House

Initiative for Educational Excellence for African-Americans", and "Distinguished Service Award" from Leadership Arlington.

Seventh, you will be a featured and keynote speaker at notable conferences.

Eighth, you will be admitted to a doctoral program.

Ninth, you will have countless impacts and connections that will positively affect many lives.

Tenth, you will submit paperwork to be promoted to full professor at a college you left over twenty years ago while on academic probation.

So, based on these upcoming accomplishments, do you really want to give-up on life and the possibility to make meaningful contributions in the world?!

The fight that you will have tomorrow is not just for you! Your fight is also for all those who are waiting for you, your work, and to learn about your story. You can't stop fighting for your beliefs, as these are the things that others want and can use to sustain their own fight.

Remember... each of us has a journey... and although yours is difficult... this is your journey to embrace and not surrender. Understand that your life matters! So tomorrow, during your weakest moments, think about the possibilities for the future and not the challenges of the past. You are already stronger than you ever imagined because you made it to this moment, and you can make it to another day again and again.

You will want to die tomorrow because you lost jobs, money, material things, so-called friends, and much more. These losses made you feel like a failure and worthless. However, you didn't lose the most important thing that you'll ever have... which is yourself. In the coming years, you'll learn that your value isn't tied to money, possessions, or titles. You will unequivocally know that your worth is directly aligned with your positive beliefs, the contributions you add to the human experience, and those who you inspire to believe in themselves. These individuals will have a direct example of an ability to overcome significant challenges based on your accomplishments. They will also envision that if you could overcome several severe life challenges, then they can do it, too.

Your story is one of strength and survival that wasn't built by money and possessions. You rebuilt your life based on a little belief, hope, and a desire to make a difference. Therefore, don't stop feeling this way, as your greatness is just beginning to be discovered.

I am the future you; I know the things that we can do! These current challenges are just moments in the grand scheme of life. Leverage these experiences and the knowledge gained to navigate from these challenges and work to rebuild a life that you want to live... on your terms.

With this letter, stop looking back, feeling bad about past losses, and begin to purposely move forward based on the knowledge you've gained from already overcoming so much.

Remember, you are a better man[34] because of and despite these challenges. Now, maximize these experiences to help yourself and others to be and do better, too.

Your life isn't wasted or a failure because if you're still alive then you have ample opportunities to restart, retool, and refocus. Your future is yet to be uncovered and experienced. Therefore, tomorrow, fight to be a part of it, as you are strong, loved, and valued.

---

[34] Reference this article in Appendix F: Becoming a Better Man.

The Long-Awaited Meeting with an Angel

I can't believe that it's been seven years since my public disclosure about my near-suicide on the "Maggie Linton Show" on SiriusXM in August 2014. Reflecting on it today, in August 2021, I am extremely grateful, thankful, and appreciative for my life. Yet, my journey and almost unbelievable transformations to live a purposeful life wouldn't have been accomplished without being able to muster the strength to courageously tell my story.

It was through my vulnerability and public sharing about my mental health journey that I gained the strength and resolve to live. Moreover, by directly addressing the sources of my pain, it began my recovery and redirected my life in ways I never would have imagined.

One of the best things that came from disclosures about my mental health challenges was meeting a mother (Mary Hanson) who lost her son (Brian) to suicide in February 2012. Our collective journeys began in March 2015 after she contacted me to tell me that my article "Letter to Myself the Day Before My Near-Suicide: Written a Year Later" had a significant impact on her, along with helping her to understand the way Brian might have felt during the final hours of his life.

During the six-year period after Mrs. Hanson's initial contact, we primarily corresponded by email and phone, except for our video meeting during the COVID-19 pandemic. We only met at that time, in June 2020, because neither of us wanted to wait any longer to finally (visually) visit each other (even remotely due to the risks associated with this virus).

However, in July 2021, things were better in the fight against COVID-19, as more people were vaccinated. Therefore, Mrs. Hanson and I decided to finally meet in-person.

> <u>Note:</u> Approximately two weeks before we met, we discovered that our mothers had the same birthday, which happened to be four days before we would embrace each other for the first time.

On July 31, I celebrated this incredible woman, mother, and friend whose support gave my work a greater meaning and my life a heightened purpose. As I walked down the restaurant's staircase to greet Mrs. Hanson, I was already in tears, as I had waited for this moment for a very long time.

Once she saw that I was approaching the table, we both moved quickly toward each other to embrace. Once we did, it felt as if we were two atoms colliding in space. However, I don't fully remember this amazingly beautiful moment. Nevertheless, once we physically connected, my feeling was that all was good in the world, and my journey through the darkness and back into the light was complete. These feelings didn't mean that the issues that plagued me were resolved. Although, with this amazing mother supporting me in ways that can't fully be described, I emerged from my cocoon that imprisoned me to transform into a person I didn't imagine I could be, but I'm glad that I've become.

The pictures from our meeting with the vibrant colors, smiles on our faces, and happiness that's clearly projected from our spirits portray the deep appreciation we have for having each other (as a family) in each other's lives.

Photo Credits: Yared Solomon

A few days after our first in-person meeting, we spoke on the phone to reflect on this incredible and heartfelt day. My summation for this experience and with reflections on the years that I fought for my life was... "If my life was to end today, then I would die a happy and blessed man!"

As I thought about this more in the following weeks, I understood that the horrible things that occurred that led to my near-suicide weren't about me. My story, impact, and evolution were based on the things I purposely chose to do in response to others' negative actions that drove these changes. Throughout my severe depression, I could have wallowed in my misery. However, for some reason that's inexplicable (and within days of wanting to end my life), I wanted to boldly share my story to help others.

My strength emerged by purposely being vulnerable and sharing the many lessons learned during my struggles with depression so that others didn't have to needlessly suffer similarly. The issue, oftentimes, with prolonged recovery from setbacks is not allowing our ego and pride from preventing action, which can prevent someone from seeking or getting the necessary assistance. It's still surprising to me that my life was saved by my open admissions that I was suffering and needed help. Perhaps, this mindset can help you to do the same.

For me, it's been a long seven years in which I learned so much about life, discovering my passions, purposely living, and reclaiming my happiness. One of the most valuable lessons learned is that change begins with taking one action to do something positive (no matter the size).

By summoning this courage to continue to move forward, it can lead to additional and positive actions that collectively build to create successful outcomes. Still, life will not always be good, kind, or the way we want it to be. Yet, in all the moments of our life, we must identify ways to live each part of it one moment at a time. As my brother, Johnnie, said to me as I was moments from ending my life... "Stacey, you need to get past this moment." Now, I'll say to you... if this moment isn't the way you want it to be, then do something (just one small thing) to change it to create the moment(s) that are wanted.

In reflecting on my shared journey with Mrs. Hanson, I wrote this poem to demonstrate our bond and love for each other.

Love Captured in the Dark

As I cried my tears while I was home
I always felt that I was all alone
Yet something from deep inside of me
Directed me to share my messages so others could see
I never imagined by fully showing my pain
I'd meet someone who would be a significant gain
The slim chance that our paths would meet
Strengthens the power of our amazing feat
For years we formed a bond without direct sight
This helped create a powerful connection without any light
We supported each other in powerful ways
Although, we didn't know we'd share so many days
As years went by our relationship significantly grew
Until we wanted to meet in-person after all we'd been through
However, right before we were scheduled to meet
We learned that our mothers shared birthdays which was such a treat
Learning about this incredible news

It was a definitive sign that we were meant to share more than the blues
While embracing each other for the first time
It seemed that the stars aligned for a yet to be revealed sign
A few weeks later this woman would see my mother's face
Shortly before my mom would leave this earthly place
It was as if there was a hand-off from one to another
That I knew that I gained a new earthly usherer
While I mourned the loss of my heavenly mother
My second mom picked-up the slack like no other
She helped me to strengthen my resolve
For without her love, I might have been ready to dissolve
I never imagined someone could be close to my mother's sacred place
Yet, this woman did it seamlessly with class, love, and grace
It was easy for her to do as an already loving mother
Because she needlessly lost a son to a disease like no other
She understood the incredible bond between a parent and a son
This strengthened our connection that won't be undone
It's because God blessed me from above
I now have a second mother to share my love

This poem is only a small reflection of the way I feel about this amazing woman, Mrs. Hanson. I can't imagine having to have made it through many of these years without her.

An Unexpected and Welcomed Surprise Visit

Since our only in-person meeting in July 2021, Mrs. Hanson and I haven't seen each other. Although, we have constant online communications. However, we have this ongoing joke in which I say to her, "If you keep acting up, then I'm going to...". Then, Mrs. Hanson quickly responds, "You're going to do what?! Go ahead and say it... make my day!" The completion of my sentence that she wanted is "... come up there."

In late June 2023, I knew that I would be traveling to the New England area. So, I checked the driving distance between the location I planned to stay and Mrs. Hanson's residence. Happily, I discovered that it wasn't a long drive. Therefore, I arranged "Operation Surprise Visit".

Shortly before I arrived in New England, I asked Mrs. Hanson if she would be home the following week for a delivery. She confirmed that she would be at home. Then, the day of my surprised arrival, I verified that Mrs. Hanson would be home that day. With her confirmation, I began to drive to her residence. Around the same time, as part of my plan, I told her that I needed to confirm if the driver was available for an afternoon delivery. The thing she didn't know was that the driver was me.

Later that day, I called Mrs. Hanson to ask if her delivery had arrived. She said that it hadn't been delivered. As I was on the phone with her, I asked her to check again just to make sure. She confirmed that there wasn't a delivery. Then, I asked her to double check. As she was checking, she said, "There's someone pulling into my driveway now." I didn't say anything. As she looked at the car and the driver getting out of it, Mrs. Hanson recoiled, and her mouth dropped to the ground. At this moment, she realized that I made a surprise visit to see her. This was one of the best moments of my life!

Photo Credits: S. L. Young

It's interesting the way in which two strangers who were privately suffering found each other to develop an incredible bond. In 2014, I purposely decided to publicly share my story to heal myself and help others. In 2015, Mrs. Hanson contacted me to share information about the loss of her son. She communicated to me via email that my article on The Huffington Post helped her to understand the way in which her son might have felt prior to him sadly ending his life.

By us bravely sharing our stories with each other, we formed a special bond that allowed us to support each other's healing. As in many things, there's strength in being vulnerable and seeking others to share that you're in pain. Neither of us could have imagined that an email exchange in March 2014 would become the gateway to an incredible bound that helped us to slowly transform, which has allowed us to truly turn darkness into light.

Parting Thoughts: Part Two

I've spent many years reflecting on and learning from the painful lessons that caused my mental health to decline. These reflections are important, but life shouldn't be spent living in the past. The future is in front of us. It's built and defined by individual moments. My focus is there and on leveraging these moments to create the future I want to purposely live... *one moment at a time.*

During the last nine years since I nearly ended my life, and the many years before that I felt increasing worthless, I never imagined that I would once again feel true happiness and joy. Well, in March 2023 and May 2023, I successfully defended my dissertation and attended my commencement as. Dr. S. L. Young, respectively.

Photo Credit: Ken Fife

Photo Credits: Maureen Bell

Without my faith, belief, hope, courage, resilience, perseverance, and resolve, I wouldn't have made it to this incredible and life-changing moment. So, in sharing the lows and highs of my life, I truly hope that it helps you to summon the strength to "choose to stay" one more day. Many times, challenges can seem to be insurmountable; I get it. However, the thing that I forgot during my depressive storm that led to me nearly and unnecessarily ending my life is (as my brother Johnnie) said to me, "Stacey, this is a just a moment; you need to get past this moment."

Therefore, before this book is ended again, I leave you with this thought to remember...

No one has failed until death, and even that's questionable.

We must remember that the work completed during our lives has an ability to impact others' existence long after our time in the physical world is done. Therefore, accomplish all that you can until there isn't time left to do or give any more. If this is mindset is applied, then you shouldn't have to look back on your life with regrets or woulda, coulda, shoulda reflections.

I hope that the information shared throughout this book helps you to be and do better, too. I wish you all the best on your journey, and I hope that all your positive wishes and dreams come true!

And always remember to…

Be your best!

****

And, before you go… please watch this video of me being introduced the first time as Dr. S. L. Young. This video was recorded almost exactly nine years from the day I nearly ended my life. This is a demonstrable example that happiness can return to your life even after going through challenging times.

youtu.be/XhmlUlh6Af8

Also, please listen to my song "Choose to Stay". This song will hopefully provide you or someone you love encouragement to hold on one more day.

youtu.be/OAmHhZwiV_Y

And finally, please watch this heartfelt and extremely emotional moment in which I thanked my brother, Johnnie, for saving my life.

youtu.be/6y2kEcjES4Q

APPENDICES

APPENDIX A:
Laws Protect Certain Classes From Workplace Abuse: Why Not Everyone?

Many individuals don't realize that workplace bullying is legal in most states and jurisdictions in the U.S., unless the actions or behaviors are so blatant that a target seeks protection under Title VII of the Civil Rights Act of 1964, which prohibits discrimination based on an individual's race, color, religion, sex, or national origin… and later amended to include pregnancy in 1978.

Federal employment laws protect individuals from workplace bullying, harassment, or abuse if (and only if) the behavior is discriminatory based on an individual being part of a protected class.

Conversely, anyone who isn't part of a protected class doesn't (as a matter of law) have the same federal protections from any arbitrary or capricious workplace bullying actions or behaviors. Therefore, individuals must rely on a company's policy (if available) or personal courage to address any hostile workplace issues. Otherwise, individuals might not be shielded from unnecessary, unwanted, or preventable attacks.

<u>Gaps in legal protections that don't protect everyone equally can lead to:</u>

- <u>disparate treatment</u> – different application of actions or behaviors to individuals under similar circumstances;

- <u>actions or behaviors taken to the limits of a law</u> – attacks might be taken far enough as to not violate Title VII or similar protections;

- <u>unprotected individuals</u> – those who aren't protected by the operation of law, company policy, or human decency.

Laws must protect everyone equally and define legally acceptable standards of behaviors, which should be applied consistently. Furthermore, legislative employment protections should set minimum standards that apply to everyone and every company; however, additional protections can and should be available to any group that doesn't have a record of equal protection under the law.

Federal and state employment laws should be developed to protect all resources (e.g., employees, contractors, temporary) from workplace bullying and companies from allegations of unfair treatment via clearly defined expectations for acceptable standards of behavior.

Company policies must be implemented and consistently applied to minimize any concerns related to other factors (e.g., disparate treatment, circumventing the law, all-star employee exceptions) that might impact compliance. Notwithstanding the availability of laws and company policies, societies have a responsibility to establish and demonstrate its permissible behavioral standards; otherwise, unnecessary abusive behavior and attacks can and will continue.

The starting point for acceptable behavior begins with each person making a choice and taking action to not allow anyone (including themselves) to be harassed, intimidated, or threatened. Anyone who allows bullying actions or behaviors to go unchallenged is complicit and deprives someone from their rights to have a quality-of-life that isn't hindered... specifically the rights to peace and an enjoyment of life.

Everyone (as documented in the Declaration of Independence) has... "... certain unalienable Rights, that among these are Life, Liberty, and the pursuit of Happiness." Therefore, Federal and state lawmakers must take swift and decisive action to safeguard individuals who otherwise can't or don't protect themselves.

Additional information on workplace bullying can be obtained in Dr. Young's solution-oriented books Bullies... They're In Your Office, Too: Could you be one? or his mini-book Management Spotlight: Workplace Bullying.

APPENDIX B:
Belief: An Underutilized Tool

There are many life lessons taught every day, such as ways to deal with others, subject matter expertise, and learning basic survival skills. However, there isn't enough time allocated to teach individuals about the power of belief. This is surprising because belief is often a cornerstone of success. Moreover, if individuals don't believe in themselves, then the reason that others should believe in their activities or causes might not be as great.

Belief is a thought, feeling, or an internal drive that can be used to overcome an obstacle, advance toward a goal, or move beyond past challenges... sometimes despite overwhelming odds. Belief isn't required to move forward. Although, it's an important tool to help summon the energy to persevere during difficult moments or challenging times. Furthermore, the biggest benefit of possessing belief is that it supports something that is significant to someone, even if nobody else agrees with it.

Belief is something that is true to an individual, very personal, needs to be developed, and can be a powerful tool for personal development. It's also a characteristic that can help individuals move forward, solve an issue, or to achieve a goal. Nevertheless, everyone doesn't have belief in themselves or may choose not to leverage their belief system to maximize their potential. Some reasons that belief might not be fully utilized are self-doubt, fear, or others' opinions. Notwithstanding, a significant reason that belief isn't used more often is that life experiences greatly influence an individual's ability to believe.

Things that happen during someone's lifetime effect their perspective and outlook. If an individual has had positive experiences associated with their beliefs, then their outlook is usually more positive. Conversely, if an individual has had bad experiences associated with their beliefs, then their outlook might be more negative. Although, a single bad experience won't always impact someone's outlook, unless an individual learns to SEE; that is, the individual experiences a (S)ignificant (E)motional (E)vent.

Once an individual begins to SEE, there is a realization (temporary or long-term) that something that was once believed to be unimportant is actually important or something that was believed to be important might not be as significant.

There are several components of belief:

- concept – an individual envisions a way to accomplish a task, activity, or project, which doesn't need to be fully understood for an idea to be developed;

- consideration – something is evaluated as a possibility, but hasn't been selected as a viable option;

- convenience – something that is used, done, or believed only if there is a potential benefit to an individual's position, situation, or desired outcome.

Oftentimes, belief might not be used sufficiently because of a lack of confidence, questionable arrogance, or a negative roadblock. Therefore, belief must be developed and maintained to achieve an internal balance that will support their goals, which includes an ability to be positive in their actions, to not be confident in a condescending manner, and to prevent any self-defeating activities that might prevent themselves or others from making forward-progress.

Belief can be a challenge because no matter the amount that someone wants something to be true. There aren't any guarantees that a belief is correct, achievable, plausible, possible, reasonable, or viable. As a result, belief requires faith in something that (many times) cannot be proven to be achievable or attainable at the time it's pursued.

Other challenges with the development of belief are that individuals:

- have doubts;
- don't have others' support;
- aren't confident in their own capabilities;
- have a need for approval;
- haven't solidified their belief;
- have a fear that prevents a pursuit of something that might be true.

Belief helps to provide energy to complete something that someone wants to achieve. However, anyone who doesn't believe in something that is thought, done, or pursued can give-up long before the desired outcome is achieved. For this reason, individuals must understand that belief isn't required to accomplish something; although, belief can be a significant factor between experiencing success or failure.

Activities that can help develop belief:

- Work on a dream despite fears, which sometimes requires moving past personal limitations and barriers to develop an idea or to achieve a desired outcome.

- Consider an idea to be in-progress and build on it.

- Act as if there isn't a possibility of failure.

- Continue to be self-motivated, even if there are setbacks.

- Minimize doubts and worries to maximize opportunities for success.

- Learn a lot from each effort, even if the outcome isn't as desired or expected.

Beliefs might not always be realized. However, individuals who don't pursue positive beliefs can limit their opportunities and options, along with minimizing their possibilities for a better future for themselves and others.

Remember… no matter the length of your journey, always be your best.

Additional information on the development of belief can be obtained in Dr. Young's solution-oriented book Management Spotlight: Belief.

APPENDIX C:
The Presentation that Changed and Saved My Life

Shortly after my near-suicide, I gave a presentation on Belief: A Powerful Component of Success[35], which was one of the most important and toughest things I've ever done, especially a couple of weeks after almost ending my life.

By delivering a happy presentation, I took active steps to move my life forward. If I was going to convince an audience to believe and take steps toward a better life, I had to believe it myself. Therefore, I used all my internal strength that day to summon happiness during my presentation. By being happy (even artificially), pushing forward, and forcing myself to truly consider the power of belief. I (in a backwards kind of way) started to convince and teach myself to believe in the value of life again.

My belief presentation helped me immensely, I hope that it will help you or anyone else who needs it, too.

---

[35] Recording of the presentation "Belief: A Powerful Component of Success" is available at: slyoung.com/power-of-belief

APPENDIX D:
Are You Really Who You Think You Are?!

Individuals often rush through the world to complete activities each day to get through their daily lives; many times, running so fast that there isn't sufficient time to slow down and ask: Who am I; what am I doing; am I really who I think I am?

The last question "Am I really who I think I am?" is a question that I never thought I would ask myself. However, once some impactful moments arrived, I was forced to ask myself the other questions: Who am I; what am I doing?

It's sometimes said that opportunities are missed because someone isn't actively looking for something that's wanted. Although, if an unexpected event, choice, or outcome occurs, these moments can sometimes force an individual to stop, take notice, and sometimes change direction. It's in these moments that an individual often learns to SEE; that is, an individual experiences a (S)ignificant (E)motional (E)vent that forces a self-examination of their own reality. Then, after experiencing growth by learning to SEE, individuals sometimes begin to ask themselves tough questions about the things that are or aren't believed to be.

<u>These reflective questions (related to an individual's decision making) are based on three perspectives:</u>

- <u>Mental</u> – decisions made based on thoughts about the elements under evaluation, such as the factors of, the considerations about, and the impact of an individual's choices. These decisions can be more difficult due to over-thinking, analyzing too much, or being convinced to believe something that isn't in alignment with an individual's beliefs;

- Emotional – choices made based on an affecting response can cause a decision to be adversely impacted due to heightened sensory stimulation. These decisions can challenge an individual's ability to distance their feelings from external stimuli;

- Spiritual – the mental and emotional perspectives can cause an individual to toil over their life's direction, because an individual's activities normally reflect their spirit and core beliefs. Moreover, an individual's core beliefs are often used to minimize opportunities for their mental or emotional perspectives from unnecessarily overriding their values.

Any individual who uses the convenience of a situation to justify any action and/or behavior that doesn't align with their supposed core beliefs must question the conviction of their beliefs as core beliefs aren't situational. However, there may be times that an individual's core beliefs are redefined based on new discoveries, corrections to previous opinions, or purposeful decisions to change their viewpoints. Despite these potential adjustments, core beliefs aren't as fluid as opinions which can change rapidly from one moment to the next.

In training for my professional career, there was never a conversation or a consideration about the possibility that I might need to make decisions that would cause me to choose between standing firm in my beliefs or being a party (willing or not) to questionable and/or unethical activities. Furthermore, none of my extensive training prepared me for the heart-wrenching decisions that were required to choose between remaining at a job and a conflict with my core beliefs that might impact my earning potential.

The easiest thing to do while faced with moral, ethical, spiritual, or other challenges is to ignore the activities of others and convince yourself that others' questionable and/or unethical activities aren't any of your concern.

During the times I encountered these types of situations, these incidents made me question myself and my beliefs. Specifically, are my beliefs really true to me; are my beliefs situational in nature; are my beliefs[36] reflective of who I am or who I want to be? The answer I sought was in this last question.

By making tough decisions during challenging times these circumstances made me truly examine not just the example I set externally, but also the standard that I set for myself internally. The external example is easy to fake and often individuals do to appease others, to cover their actions, or to receive a personal benefit... even though I didn't in these situations.

The internal example isn't as easy to fake, move past, or convince yourself that it's actually true. Unlike the external projection, the internal projection might be personally impactful long after a current situation. Therefore, will you

---

[36] Reference this article in Appendix B: Belief – An Underutilized Tool.

act and/or behave a certain way for others, but then continue to toil over some of the worst disappointment possible... to yourself?

Some of the hardest things that an individual can do during their lifetime are to live with the outcome of their actions, behaviors, choices, or decisions. For this reason, does it not make sense that an individual ensures that their spiritual, emotional, and mental perspectives/decisions are aligned?

The answer to this last question isn't for me to provide for others; however, my hope is that this question is something individuals will thoughtfully consider.

Additional information on the development of belief can be obtained in Dr. Young's solution-oriented book Management Spotlight: Belief.

APPENDIX E:
Why Shouldn't Men Cry?!

Individuals often rush through the world to complete activities each day to get through their daily lives; many times, running so fast that there isn't sufficient time to slow down and ask: Who am I; what am I doing; am I really who I think I am?

Crying is something that everyone does; it's a normal part of life. However, if you're male, then there are often different standards applied. The issue is that too many times and unnecessarily some people associate men crying with being weak, effeminate, or gay. The projection conveyed is that a man is somehow less than whole if any or too much emotion is displayed.

In January 2016, there was plenty of commentary about President Obama's public display of emotion (shedding a tear) while discussing gun violence in the United States (U.S.). The questions that immediately emerged were related to whether it's appropriate for a country's leader to display emotion. These comments were made as if being emotional or crying would somehow diminish the power of or respect for the man and the office. An alternative view is that it represents caring and compassion, along with a display of a lack of ego, strength, confidence, and self-awareness.

Anyone who is comfortable with themselves doesn't worry about others' perceptions about their self-expression. The challenge is that others (through judgments) will transfer their fears, worries, and doubts about the way a man who cries is perceived.

A couple of men known for openly and unabatedly crying are John Boehner (former speaker of the U.S. House of

Representatives) and Steve Harvey. Speaker Boehner would (at times) become very emotional while discussing issues that were meaningful to him and Steve Harvey has lost his composure a few times on his talk show, especially while discussing his wife, family, or past. Both men aren't weakened by their public display of emotions; instead, these are the moments that each connected further with their vulnerability, feelings, and humanity.

Personally, I don't like to cry, but I'm not afraid or embarrassed to do it either. The first lesson I learned about the proper display of a man's emotions was at my grandmother's funeral. At the service, a man in my family corrected me for crying; his words and actions basically told me to man-up. During this service, my emotions overflowed for the loss of my grandmother who I: loved very much, lived with for a while, and directly experienced the death of a family member for the first time. My response to this correction was direct, assertive, and purposeful. This moment wasn't about maintaining superficial experiences or expressions. This moment was about my grandmother, my moment to grieve, and a part of my healing process. If I didn't allow myself to grieve as it happened, then I might not have adequately coped with her death or prolonged the healing process.

An example of my reluctance to cry was in my college classroom while students provided some positive feedback. In that moment, I started to become emotional, but I didn't allow myself to cry. Instead, I joked about the temperature rising in the classroom and quickly fanned my eyes to prevent from releasing a tear. By blocking my emotions and feelings, I missed an opportunity to fully experience the happiness and joy that could have resulted from an unabashed connection with these moments.

Crying is important because it:
- releases pain;
- helps individuals to heal;
- isn't a sign of a weakness;
- allows feelings of happiness to be fully realized;
- is a normal part of life.

In discussing men crying with friends on Facebook, a few commented as follows:

- So much relief and release can be achieved! (Kwang Kim);

- It's not healthy if you don't cry; screw what other people think! And so what if I might break out in tears for reasons others might not be aware. Who cares; who are they to judge?! And I dare anyone to question my manhood! We need to stop using double standards and try to understand each other. (Robert Meredith);

- It's such an easy way to release stress; let go of anger and pent-up emotions and just simply feel. And once you do it (for even a few minutes) the relief you feel is amazing. You don't have to prove yourself by doing it in front of others. Cry by yourself; it's still therapeutic. I'm really proud of my husband. He's a big strong guy who allows himself to cry whenever he feels strongly. It might be a touching story on ESPN or the news. I respect him so much for that and interestingly trust him even more for it. (Dawn Leach Gaskill).

If crying wasn't a normal, biological process, then it wouldn't happen as an uncontrolled response. The process that isn't normal is to block crying because doing so prevents someone from experiencing a natural response and having an emotional release. The alternative is to suppress feelings by not addressing or blocking them, but inevitably unresolved emotional or psychological issues will be released in other forms (e.g., use of alcohol/drugs, a mental breakdown, abusive behavior, even worse death/suicide).

APPENDIX F:
Becoming A Better Man

In 2014, I called one of my brothers to ask a very important question, "If anything happens to me, will you take care of ma?" My goal was to obtain confirmation for my question and then end my life, but it didn't go as planned. I began to cry, my brother started to ask questions, and then I abruptly hung-up the phone. Then, over the next hour, my brother franticly called to attempt to contact and help me.

On that cold March morning, I almost died-by-suicide because I falsely believed that I didn't have any value, and no one wanted the things I did. Also, I thought, "If being ethical caused this much pain and torment, then… why would I want to live anymore?! Even though I was ready and prepared to end my life, I didn't want to die. However, I desperately wanted the emotional pain to end with the quickest path to relief.

Over a few years in different organizations, I fought against being complicit to unethical activities. The requests and directions I received (as a consultant) were surprising and shocking. In over a decade of working at Fortune 500 companies (while managing multi-million dollar projects), I was almost never asked to do anything I believed to be ethically and/or morally wrong. Notwithstanding, I did witness bad decision-making. Although, this isn't the same as intentional actions for personal gain.

At one company, after delivering independent audit results for a state government client, I was asked to change information in a report to justify an organization's desire for additional funding. After discussing this request with my company's executive team, the decision made was that the report wouldn't be changed. Then, the client threatened to no longer do business with this small consulting company if the report didn't reflect its wishes. Shortly thereafter, my leadership team directed me to alter the report to meet the client's needs, which I refused to do because the changes didn't reflect my documented findings.

In another organization, I contracted for a federal government client. Every day I requested work to do, but I wasn't assigned any tasks to complete. My requests continued for weeks (while being paid to sit at my desk) until I was finally directed to develop a project budget. Upon requesting verifiable budget information from the project's executive, I was directed to enter whatever costs I wanted to input without any information to substantiate the forecast. After this incident, being continuously underemployed, and being asked to engage in unethical activities, I sought other employment.

There was another incident in which I was constantly belittled, scolded, and essentially called "stupid" several times. After reporting these incidents to my executive manager, the hostile and unprovoked attacks didn't abate. As a result, I couldn't justifiably continue to work for an organization in which I was disrespected, demeaned, and devalued.

After a period of short assignments, I couldn't obtain gainful employment. As the months and years passed, my drive to succeed deteriorated, my future earning potential was highly uncertain, I lost hope, and I was extremely depressed. These pressures led to the day I almost ended my life.

The primary things that saved my life were: (1) my brother

telling me, "Stacey, this is a just a moment; you need to get past this moment.", and (2) going to the Arlington County Detention Facility (ACDF) a few hours after I almost died-by-suicide to teach inmates. At the detention facility, surprisingly, I couldn't enter that day because it was on lockdown. Nevertheless, by mustering the courage to go there, I took affirmative action to begin to reclaim my life and drive my future.

The ironic thing is that teaching inmates isn't something I ever wanted to do. Yet, my friends and family convinced me to do it, along with suggesting that my inspirational books should be used with this population. Interestingly, my time at the jail teaching incarcerated individuals made me forget my personal troubles that kept me in a depressive state. Being in this environment and teaching these men gave me a renewed sense of purpose, meaningful work, and value.

I wrote this quote during my darkest days to help remind me about the importance of forward-progress:

> *Your darkest days don't define you, but instead provide an opportunity for you to display your strength and character, which will ultimately drive the individual you become.*

There can be other plans for our lives that are communicated in sometimes subtle messages that can be missed if we're not open to receiving them. These messages can validate our existence, journey, and path.

During my first ACDF visit to determine if I could teach at a jail, something surprising happened. As I entered the housing unit in which I would teach, unexpectedly someone yelled my name. At first, I ignored it because I didn't know anyone at this jail. Then, I heard my name again, which was directed toward me by someone I didn't recognize. After getting my attention, I was reminded that we were friends in high school. This experience changed my perspective about teaching inmates because I connected to a common bond of humanity, reflected on the significance of this chance encounter, and accepted my outreach with humility.

Another one of my quotes that helped strengthen my will was:

> *Many individuals are afraid of jail; however, individuals often lock themselves in their own prisons. Be your own warden and set yourself free of unnecessary worry, doubts, and limitations.*

My heart-wrenching choices taught me powerful lessons about living a purposeful life:

- First, fighting to do the right things and making positive changes is always beneficial even if the short-term pain might seem unbearable;

- Second, current circumstances might affect me, but it doesn't need to define my future unless I choose to unnecessarily surrender;

- Third, even during the worst moments, I can support others while at the same time helping myself;

- Fourth, wasting time engaging in self-deprecating behavior or destructive activities will only hurt myself while not improving my current situation;

- Fifth; there's an immeasurable value in not needlessly losing yourself to conform to others' self-serving interests.

I humbly learned throughout these experiences that with positive, definitive choices (while confronting unimaginable circumstances and overwhelming odds), I won't ever need to wonder if I did the right things. This mentality will allow me to intentionally create the life "I purposely choose to live."

Learn about Dr. Young's work to raise awareness about the impacts of harassment and workplace bullying: slyoung.com/workplace-bullying

APPENDIX G:
Inmate Management: What's Wanted Better Criminals or Citizens?

An ability to access a quality education is an important factor in the achievement of educational success and a benefit of being part of a civilized nation. A scientific study isn't required to understand that individuals who don't have access to quality educational options (or maximize their opportunities) can be negatively impacted throughout their lives by underemployment, income gaps, stress, depression, incarceration, and more.

In May 2014, Brookings Institute experts Melissa S. Kearney and Benjamin H. Harris released the "Hamilton Project Policy Memo[37]" that included analysis about the impacts of the lack of educational achievement. Part of its focus was to determine if any relationship(s) existed between educational levels and incarceration rates. In this memo, ten economic facts were used to highlight crime and incarceration trends in the United States (U.S.).

<u>Much of this information is jarring, but a couple of the points in the memo are very troubling:</u>

- <u>Fact 7</u> – There is nearly a 70 percent chance that an African American man without a high school diploma will be imprisoned by his mid-thirties;

- <u>Fact 8</u> – Per capita expenditures on corrections more than tripled over the past thirty years.

The rest of this piece will first focus on the impact of black

---

[37] This memo can be reviewed at: hamiltonproject.org/publication/economic-fact/ten-economic-facts-about-crime-and-incarceration-in-the-united-states/

educational levels compared to projected future incarceration rates. Then, there will be consideration about the impact of improving educational opportunities for all inmates.

The first fact that a black man who doesn't earn his high school diploma has a 70% chance of being imprisoned by his mid-thirties is dumbfounding. In Shara Tonn's Stanford Report (News) article "Stanford Research Suggests Support for Incarceration Mirrors Whites' Perception of Black Prison Populations"[38], published in the Stanford News (August 2014), she wrote, "Although African-Americans constitute only 12 percent of America's population, they represent 40 percent of the nation's prison inmates." These statistics alone should cause many to ask probing questions about the reasons that this is true and the message it sends about a nation that allows such blatant disparities.

If education is a key component of future personal and economic success, then why isn't more being done to help everyone achieve it? Is it the lack of caring, politics, educational system failures, systemic racism, or a combination of all these things? Regardless of the reasons for these abysmal outcomes, these issues are humanitarian issues and societal failures; the good news is that systematic adjustments can be implemented to drive immediate and actionable changes.

The second fact that corrections expenses on a per capita basis have more than tripled over the past thirty years is disheartening. Have we as a nation decided that lives aren't

---

[38] Stanford Report (August 2014): news.stanford.edu/news/2014/august/prison-black-laws-080614.html (was previously available using this link)

worth saving and the best option is to increase expenditures on housing, feeding, and storing U.S. citizens? Isn't one of the goals of a civilized nation to create opportunities to ensure that everyone has a realistic probability to achieve life, liberty, and the pursuit of happiness?

What if funding was redirected from correctional spending to infrastructure to support innovative, developmental solutions for educational advancements? The positive impact on high school graduation rates and the negative impact on the number of incarcerations would be worthwhile improvements that can positively change lives. The other potential benefits of educational funding and development are increased income levels, better employment opportunities, and a better chance for an improved quality of life. By shifting funding to proactive and diversion programs instead of investing in detention and retention, greater possibilities exist for economic, societal, and personal benefits.

I've observed the negative impacts of incarceration (e.g., hopelessness, lack of motivation, feelings of rejection, dejection) through the aftermaths of family, friends, and inmates I've taught serving non-productive time. None of these individuals said to me "I'm better because of the experience." Some might be thinking now… "It's their own fault; jail isn't supposed to be fun." Even though these thoughts might be true, continually having punitive consequences without providing career pathways toward a better future isn't a viable option either.

The biggest challenge with not providing inmates with meaningful educational options and opportunities is that money is spent primarily on maintaining the system versus providing educational nutrients. Furthermore, a considerable amount of an inmate's time is spent in a suspended state waiting for release. The worst potential outcomes are that inmates without sufficient mental engagement will become hardened and/or learn methods to become more sophisticated criminals. As a result, the societal costs can exceed the three-fold increase in correctional expenditures over the last thirty years.

The inmates I've worked with want purposeful educational training[39]. These inmates tell me that having a variety of programs is great; however, many want to have classes that lead to good employment opportunities after incarceration. One of the biggest life-altering changes and realizations that too many inmates with felony convictions experience after incarceration are significantly reduced chances for gainful employment. These types of career and life limiters are slowly changing as the result of initiatives like 'ban the box'. Notwithstanding, a criminal record coupled with a felony conviction can translate into an ongoing punishment. If skill development, career training, or life skills management aren't provided while inmates are incarcerated, what additional motivation will inmates have to live better lives after their release? There must be an availability of transitional educational and career opportunities to reduce the possibility of former inmates becoming habitual offenders.

In the programs offered to inmates through my nonprofit organization "Saving Our Communities at Risk Through Educational Services (SOCARTES - socartes.org)", inmates

---

[39] Learn more about Dr. Young's work: slyoung.com/inspired

tell me that the training offered assists with their personal development by teaching them valuable lessons about life, business, and soft skills. Therefore, an ability to maximize the time these inmates spend on purposeful versus recreational activities will greatly increase the probability of their success after incarceration. The unfortunate reality is that too many inmates aren't offered developmental, educational programs that will maximize their time to become better citizens instead of better criminals.

<u>In my current program at the Arlington County Detention Facility in Arlington, VA, inmates told me:</u>

- "It's important to have positive avenues to use the time in a positive manner. Not only for teaching productive knowledge in a negative environment, but to also create a platform in which individuals can build a foundation that they can continue to build on once released. Otherwise jails will perpetuate criminology which old cons will teach new cons." (J. Scorza);

- "It is vital for mental growth and stability, further advancement instead of being idle. I take all programs to further my knowledge and widen my brain so that I don't limit myself." (D. Messiha);

- "Occupies inmates' time in a positive manner. The general concern of many of them is the re-entry process. Many look forward to classes that cover topics that can be used in the real world." (M. Reyes).

Increasing spending on detention and retention isn't the answer to the growing gaps in educational inequality that leads to increased incarcerations (generally and for black men specifically). It's beyond time that funding is used for proactive initiatives that focus on the reduction of the needlessly increasing rates of incarceration. Furthermore, minimal investments in community-based organizations and diversion programs can have priceless effects, along with significant impacts that can reduce the school-to-prison pipeline. Moreover, focus on the cost to educate and not incarcerate is the best method to prevent the cycle of mass incarcerations that's clearly not working. If meaningful change is wanted, then radical efforts are needed because the current, outdated solutions have proved to be highly ineffective, costly, and damaging to too many lives… for inmates and society.

About the Author

Dr. S. L. Young is an author, professor, career coach, former HuffPost contributor, founder of the educational non-profit organization "Saving Our Communities at Risk Through Educational Services (SOCARTES – socartes.org)", founder of the for-profit company "Beyond SPRH, LLC – beyondsprh.com)", and former host of "Beyond Just Talk with S. L. Young". The topics of his books include belief, communication, negotiation, time management, workplace bullying, ethics, overcoming challenges, and inspirational quotes.

In 2012, Dr. Young became an author with the release of his first book in the "It's a Crazy World… Learn From It" series.

Dr. Young graduated from the American University in Washington, D.C. with a Bachelor of Science in Business Administration (B.S.B.A.) degree in International Business with a marketing concentration. He also graduated from The George Washington University in Washington, D.C. with two degrees: Master of Business Administration (M.B.A.) in Finance and Investments with a human resources concentration and a Master of Science (M.S.) in Project Management. In 2023, at Marymount University, he successfully defended his Doctorate (Ed.D.) in Educational Leadership and Organizational Innovation. The focus of his doctoral research was "Student Engagement's Impact on Academic Performance for Nontraditional Students in a Community College Environment".

In 2022, Dr. Young was inducted into and became a life member of The Honor Society of Phi Kappa Phi. In 2023, he was inducted into The Honor Society of Kappa Delta Pi.

Additionally, he's a life-member of the professional business fraternity of Alpha Kappa Psi.

Dr. Young's professional career includes approximately fifteen years with Fortune 500 companies, including Bell Atlantic, MCI, Sprint Nextel, and various consulting engagements, in the areas of billing, customer service, engineering, finance, information technology, network security, operations, product development, and software quality assurance.

Dr. Young, for nearly fifteen years, has taught a variety of classes (i.e., Introduction to Business, Entrepreneurship, Business Communication, Marketing, Small Business Management, Organizational Behavior, and Principles of Management at the Northern Virginia Community College. He previously taught at Marymount University for nearly four years.

In 2012, Dr. Young created his nonprofit organization "Saving Our Communities at Risk Through Educational Services (SOCARTES)" to share life and business lessons with individuals in opportunity "at-risk" communities. Through his work with SOCARTES, he created additional pathways for him to give-back to and make meaningful connections in various communities.

Dr. Young's passion to help others is fueled based on his abilities to excel academically and professionally. These accomplishments occurred after being directed to leave high school in tenth grade, graduating in the bottom 8% of his high school class, and leaving several colleges prior to becoming actively engaged in the process of learning. These experiences drove his desires to tirelessly help others in meaningful ways and various environments.

In January 2015, Dr. Young launched his for-profit business "(Beyond SPRH, LLC)", which provides solution-oriented services to help individuals and organizations to maximize output potential.

In 2018, Dr. Young received special recognition for his work to educate an incarcerated population. The first was the Martin Luther King, Jr. Drum Major Innovative Service Award from the U.S. Department of Education for Faith-Based and Neighborhood Partnerships, in collaboration with the White House Initiative for Educational Excellence for African Americans. The second was the Distinguished County Service Award from Volunteer Arlington (a program of the Leadership Center for Excellence).

Dr. Young is driven to share his knowledge that leads to developmental opportunities (especially for underserved and marginalized communities). Through his authentic lived-experiences overcoming challenges, Dr. Young works tirelessly to inspire others to overcome challenges and pursue their dreams, too.

Dr. Young's published works:

- Above Expectations – My Story: an unlikely journey from almost failing high school to becoming a college professor

- Bullies...They're In Your Office, Too: Could you be one?

- Choosing To Take A Stand: Changed me, my life, and my destiny

- Ethical Opportunity Cost: It's a matter of choice

- It's a Crazy World… Learn From It:

    o Part I – Taking Care of Me

    o Part II – Moving Forward

    o Part III – Keeping It Going

    o Part IV – The Journey Continues

- Management Spotlight:

    o Belief

    o Communication

    o Critical Thinking/Thick-Skin

    o Negotiation

    o Time Management

    o Workplace Bullying

- Soft Skills Development:
    - Belief
    - Communication
    - Critical Thinking/Thick-Skin
    - Negotiation
    - Time Management
- Turning Darkness Into Light: Inspiring lessons after a near-suicide

Made in United States
Orlando, FL
01 May 2024